BSCS Science Tracks
Connecting Science and Literacy

Investigating
Human Systems

Second Edition

KENDALL/HUNT PUBLISHING COMPANY
4050 Westmark Drive   Dubuque, Iowa 52002

BSCS Staff, Second Edition

BSCS Administrative Staff
Carlo Parravano, Chair, Board of Directors
Rodger W. Bybee, Executive Director
Janet Carlson Powell, Associate Director
Pamela Van Scotter, Director, Center for Curriculum Development
Marcia L. Mitchell, Director of Finance

Project Staff
April Gardner, Deborah Jordan, Project Directors
Barbara Perrin, Director of Publications
Dottie Watkins, Production Coordinator
Stacey Luce, Manuscript Specialist, Permissions
Pamela S. Warren, Assistant to Center for Curriculum Development Director
Judy L. Rasmussen, Assistant to Center for Research and Evaluation Co-Director
Dave Somers, Colorado Springs, Colorado, Editor

Reviewers
Linda Block-Gandy, Mary McMillan Magee, Harold Pratt, Norby Pratt, Julie L. Norris
Ward's Natural Science, Safety Review

BSCS Staff, First Edition

BSCS Development Team
Nancy M. Landes, Project Director and Author, 1996–1998
Gail C. Foster, Author
Colleen K. Steurer, Author
Vonna G. Pinney, Executive Assistant
Linda K. Ward, Senior Executive Assistant
Rodger W. Bybee, Principal Investigator, 1994–1995
Harold Pratt, Project Director, 1994–1996
Janet Chatlain Girard, Art Coordinator, 1994–1996

BSCS Administrative Staff
Timothy H. Goldsmith, Chair, Board of Directors
Joseph D. McInerney, Director
Michael J. Dougherty, Assistant Director
Lynda B. Micikas, Assistant Director
Larry Satkowiak, Chief Financial Officer

Contributors and Consultants
Randall K. Backe, BSCS, Colorado Springs, Colorado, Contributing Author
Judy L. Capra, Wheat Ridge, Colorado, Freelance Writer
Michael J. Dougherty, BSCS, Colorado Springs, Colorado
B. Ellen Friedman, San Diego, California
Cathy Griswold, Lyons, Oregon, Contributing Author
Jay Hackett, Greeley, Colorado
Debra A. Hannigan, Colorado Springs, Colorado, Contributing Author
David A. Hanych, BSCS, Colorado Springs, Colorado
Karen Hollweg, Washington, DC
Winston King, Bridgetown, Barbados
Paul Kuerbis, Colorado Springs, Colorado
Donald E. Maxwell, BSCS, Colorado Springs, Colorado
Brenda S. McCreight, Colorado Springs, Colorado, Freelance Writer
Mary McMillan, Boulder, Colorado
Marge Melle, Littleton, Colorado, Freelance Writer
Lynda B. Micikas, BSCS, Colorado Springs, Colorado
Jean P. Milani, BSCS, Colorado Springs, Colorado
Renee Mitchell, Lakewood, Colorado, Freelance Writer
Janet Carlson Powell, Boulder, Colorado, Contributing Author
Carol D. Prekker, Broomfield, Colorado, Freelance Writer

ISBN 978-0-7575-1120-2

Copyright © 1999, 2006 by BSCS. All rights reserved. No part of this work may be reproduced or transmitted in any form or by any means, electronic or mechanical, including photocopying and recording, or by any information storage or retrieval system without permission in writing. For permissions and other rights under this copyright, please contact BSCS, 5415 Mark Dabling Boulevard, Colorado Springs, CO 80918.

10 9 8 7 6 5 4   10 09

Patricia J. Smith, Tucson, Arizona, Freelance Writer

Terry G. Spencer, Monterey, California, Contributing Author

Patti M. Thorn, Austin, Texas, Contributing Author

Bonnie Turnbull, Monument, Colorado, Freelance Writer

Terri B. Weber, Colorado Springs, Colorado

Carol A. Nelson Woller, Boulder, Colorado, Freelance Writer

Field-Test Teachers and Coordinators

Joanne Allen, Westport Elementary School, Westport, Maine

Helene Auger, Westport School District, Westport, Maine

Sheila Dallas, Bethany School, Cincinnati, Ohio

Pat Dobosenski, Pembroke Elementary School, Troy, Michigan

Nina Finkel, Whitter Elementary School, Chicago, Illinois

Mary Elizabeth France, Westport Elementary School, Westport, Maine

Carolyn Gardner, Calhan Elementary School, Calhan, Colorado

Shelly Gordon, Bingham Farms Elementary School, Birmingham, Michigan

Darlene Grunert, Birmingham Public Schools, Birmingham, Michigan

Terry Heinecke, Edgerton Elementary School, Kalispell, Montana

Katherine Hickey, Irving Primary School, Highland Park, New Jersey

Jan Himmelspach, Grayson Elementary School, Waterford, Michigan

Elizabeth Lankes, Bethany School, Glendale, Ohio

Barbara O'Neal, Calhan Elementary School, Calhan, Colorado

Cheryl Pez, Bethany School, Cincinnati, Ohio

Rochelle Rubin, Waterford School District-IMC, Waterford, Michigan

Elizabeth A. Smith, Grayson Elementary School, Waterford, Michigan

Melanie W. Smith, Washington Elementary School, Raleigh, North Carolina

Janet Smith-James, Bartle School, Highland Park, New Jersey

Catherine Snyder, Highland Park School District, Highland Park, New Jersey

Ingrid Snyder, Waterford Village School, Waterford, Michigan

Lee Ann Van Horn, Wake County Public School System, Raleigh, North Carolina

Kathy Wright, Calhan Elementary School, Calhan, Colorado

Reviewers

Marsha Barber, Jefferson County Public Schools, Golden, Colorado

James P. Barufaldi, University of Texas at Austin

Diane Brunner, U.S. Olympic Training Center, Colorado Springs, Colorado

Judy Capra, Jefferson County Public Schools, Golden, Colorado

Candance L. Cline, Etiwanda Elementary School, Etiwanda, California

Larry W. Esposito, University of Colorado at Boulder

Brenda S. Evans, Department of Education, Raleigh, North Carolina

Eva Filsinger, Air Academy High School, Colorado Springs, Colorado

Randy Gray, National Weather Service, Pueblo, Colorado

Leslie Hartten, University of Colorado at Boulder

Steven Holman, Salem, Oregon

Andrew Hudak, University of Colorado at Boulder

Judith Johnson, University of Central Florida, Orlando, Florida

Eric Leonard, The Colorado College, Colorado Springs, Colorado

Ted Lindeman, The Colorado College, Colorado Springs, Colorado

Brownie Linder, Northern Arizona University, Flagstaff, Arizona

Jerry Ludwig, Fox Lane High School, Bedford, New York

Michael J. Madsen, KKTV, Channel 11, Colorado Springs, Colorado

Robert T. Moline, Gustavus Adolphus College, St. Peter, Minnesota

Cherilynn A. Morrow, Space Science Institute, Boulder, Colorado

Rajul Pandya, National Center for Atmospheric Research, Boulder, Colorado

Joseph Pettit, University of Colorado at Boulder

Robert I. Pinney, Colorado Springs, Colorado

Kathleen Roth, Michigan State University, East Lansing, Michigan

Barbara W. Saigo, Saiwood Biology Resources, Montgomery, Alabama

Mary Santlemann, Oregon State University, Corvallis, Oregon

Gail Shroyer, Kansas State University, Manhattan, Kansas
David L. Smith, LaSalle University, Philadelphia, Pennsylvania
Carol Snell, University of Central Florida, Orlando, Florida
John Staver, Kansas State University, Manhattan, Kansas
Joseph Stepans, University of Wyoming, Laramie, Wyoming
Robert Steurer, U.S. West Communications, Colorado Springs, Colorado
Richard Storey, The Colorado College, Colorado Springs, Colorado
Joan Tephly, Marycrest University, Iowa City, Iowa
Lee Vierling, University of Colorado at Boulder
Jack Wheatley, North Carolina State University, Raleigh, North Carolina
Emmet Wright, Kansas State University, Manhattan, Kansas

Contents

Investigating Human Systems

Introduction	Doing Science	1
Lesson 1	Believe It or Not	23
Lesson 2	Muscles, Bones, and Fitness	39
Lesson 3	Count the Beats	55
Lesson 4	A Breathing System	77
Lesson 5	Fitness from the Inside Out	101
Lesson 6	Nutrition and Fitness	113
Lesson 7	My Plans for Fitness	131
Exercise Appendix		149
Glossary		167
Acknowledgements		173

Introduction

Doing Science

What is science? What is doing science? What do people do when they do science?

Talk about the following questions with your teammates. Then write your own response to each question in your notebook. Be prepared to discuss your ideas with the class.

1. What is science?

2. What is doing science?

3. What do people do when they do science?

4. What is a scientist like?

5. Can you be a scientist right now?

How Do You Do Science?

Have you ever wondered about anything? Have you ever asked questions about plants, animals, or things? Have you ever investigated to find the answers to your questions? If so, you were doing science! People who do science try to find answers to questions.

As people do science, they wonder and ask questions. They investigate to find answers to their questions. They use their senses and tools to collect information. They keep records as they collect information. They develop explanations to their questions based on information that they have collected. They share ideas and explanations with other people. Sometimes this process leads them to new questions, and the whole process begins again.

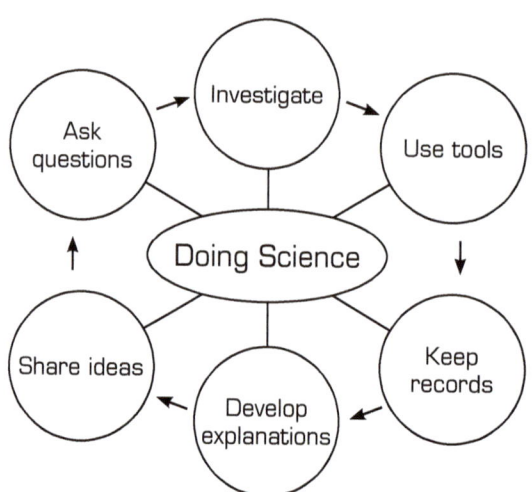

Doing Science Graphic Organizer

During this module, you will do science. You will investigate the human body, how it works, and ways to keep it healthy.

Ask Questions

Doing science starts with asking a question. People who do science wonder about the world around them. They are curious about objects, animals, plants, or things that happen in the world. What do you think scientists wonder about? What kinds of questions do you think they ask? What do you wonder about? What questions do you ask?

Science students ask questions.

Scientists ask questions.

Doing Science 3

Investigate

People who do science investigate to find answers to their questions. Sometimes they use their senses to observe things. They describe and compare the objects, materials, and living things that they are investigating. Sometimes they do something to the objects and find out what happens to them. Sometimes they do a fair test and observe what happens. What do you think the scientist in the following photograph might be investigating? What do you think you might be investigating during this module?

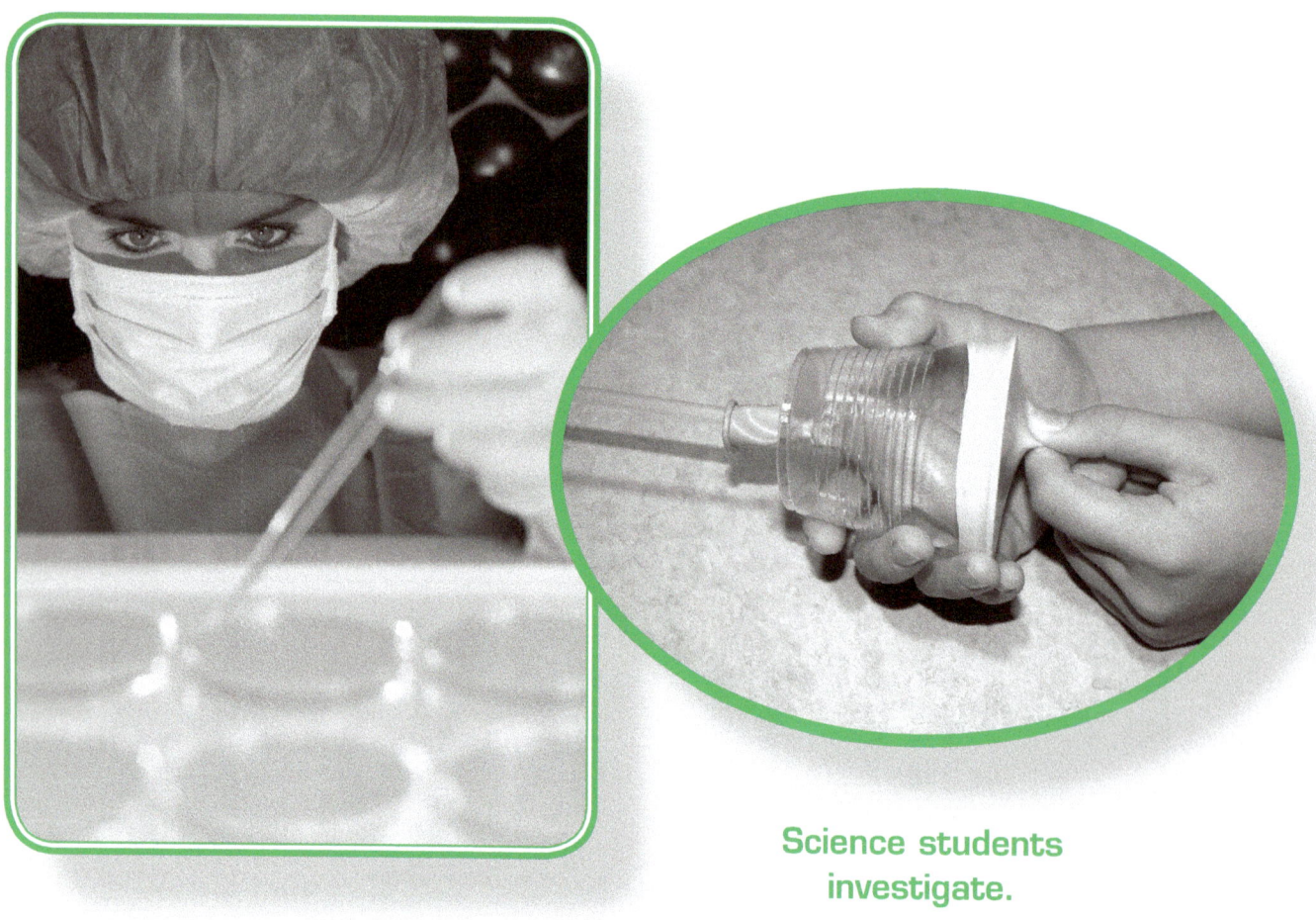

Scientists investigate.

Science students investigate.

Use Tools

People who do science use tools, such as thermometers, magnifying glasses, microscopes, and rulers. They use science tools to help them get information, or **data**, that they cannot get by using just their senses. What tool is the scientist in the following photograph using? What science tools have you used? What kinds of tools do you think you will use during this module?

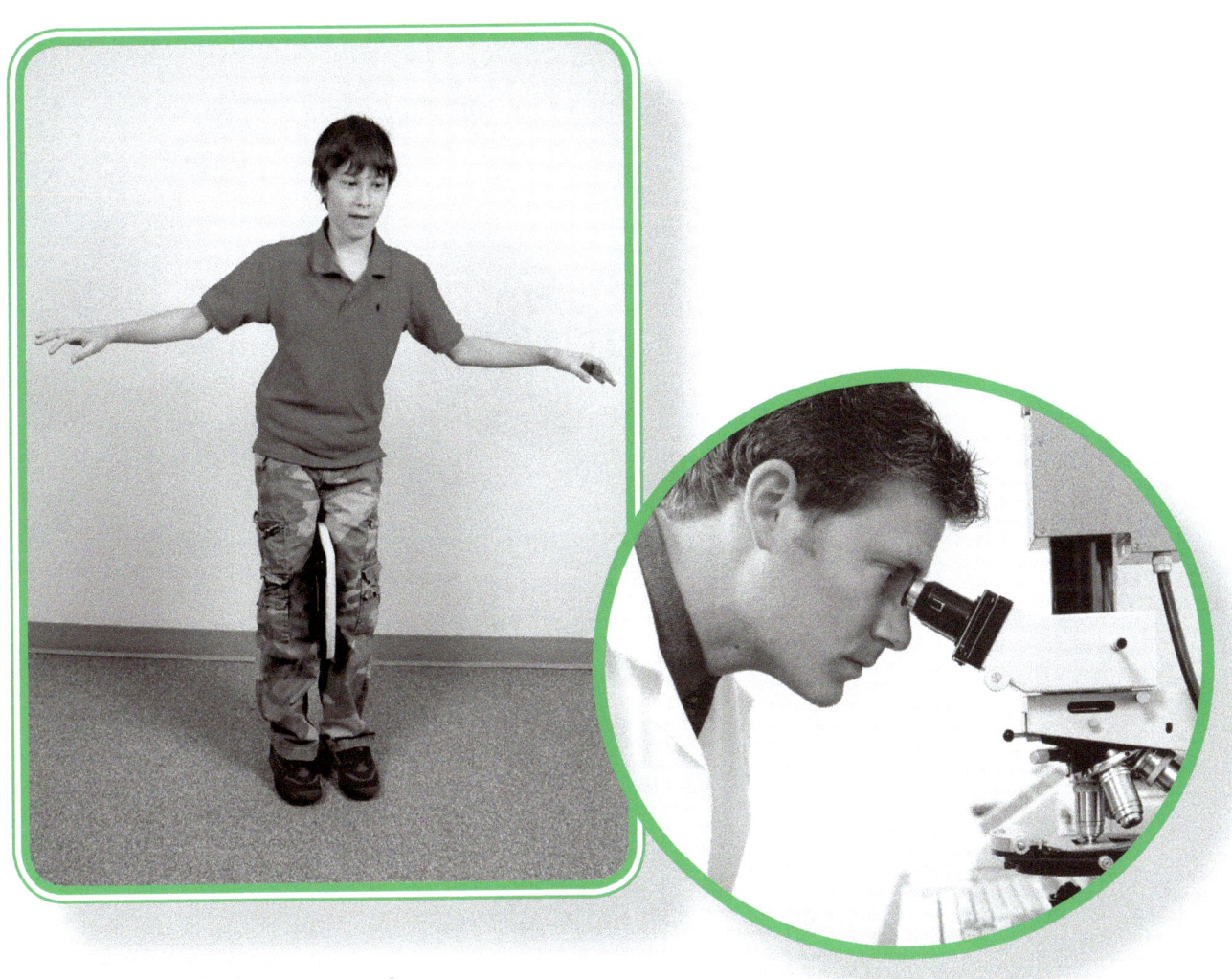

Science students use tools.

Scientists use tools.

Doing Science 5

Keep Records

People who do science document data during their investigations. They write, draw, and make charts and graphs. Scientists' documents are called **records**. Scientists compare their records with the records of other scientists. During this module, you will keep records of your investigations. How might you keep records of your investigations? You will also compare your records with the records of other students.

Science students keep records.

Scientists keep records.

Develop Explanations

One of the important jobs of people who do science is to explain how and why things happen in the world around us. People who do science explain the answers to their questions. They use the data that they have collected to develop explanations. Scientists use their records and data to develop explanations. You will use your records and data to help you explain things.

Science students develop explanations.

Scientists develop explanations.

Share Ideas

People who do science share and discuss their ideas with other people. Sometimes they do their investigations again to find out if the same thing happens another time. Sometimes other people do the same investigation. Then they compare what happened in all the investigations. Scientists share their ideas and explanations. You will share your ideas and explanations with your classmates.

Scientists share their ideas.

Science students share their ideas.

Ask New Questions

One good question leads to another. People who do science are full of questions. As scientists do investigations, they usually think of new questions that they want to answer. Then they do more investigations. Scientists never stop wondering and asking questions about why things are the way they are. We hope that your investigations during this module make you wonder and ask new questions.

Science students ask new questions.

Scientists ask new questions.

Look back at the graphic organizer on page 2 and review the process for doing science. Does the process make sense? Do you think that it is a good way to think about doing science?

Doing Science 9

Working Together to Do Science

Scientists, engineers, and other people who do science often work in teams so that they can share ideas and tasks. When you do science, you will work in teams too. Sometimes you will work with your friends. Other times, you will work with teammates you don't know as well. You may stay in the same team through several lessons. Teammates have responsibilities as they work together.

All teammates are responsible for

- doing the task well and
- helping their teammates understand the task and what the team did.

Team Skills

It is easier to do your team task well if you practice some team skills while you work. You will use the following five team skills every time you work in a team.

Team Skills

1. Move into your team quickly and quietly.
2. Stay with your team.
3. Speak softly.
4. Share and take turns.
5. Do your job.

1. **Move into your team quickly and quietly.** When your teacher tells you to meet with your team, find your teammates right away. Go directly to your team's meeting place without stopping to talk along the way.

2. **Stay with your team.** This skill means that you pay attention to your teammates and work with them to do your task. You do not wander around the room and talk to other teams.

3. **Speak softly.** When you talk with your teammates, keep your voice down so only your teammates can hear you.

4. **Share and take turns.** The skill of sharing and taking turns takes some practice. You and your teammates must make sure that everyone on the team gets to do part of each investigation and to share his or her ideas.

5. **Do your job.** When you work as a team, each teammate will be responsible for one job that helps the team (materials manager, tracker, messenger, or skill builder). You might like one job more than the others, but each job is important for the team. You will have a chance to do all the jobs at some time. The job descriptions are on pages 16–17. Whenever your teammates change jobs, review the descriptions so that everyone will remember what to do.

Special Team Skills

Sometimes your team will practice special skills that will help you work better together. Read the special skills and talk about them with your teacher. Describe what your team will say and do to practice each special skill.

■ Special Team Skills

1. Discuss many ideas before selecting one.

2. Ask questions to help you understand someone else's ideas.

3. Criticize ideas, not people.

1. **Discuss many ideas before selecting one.** Often, there are many ways to do an investigation or solve a problem. Using this skill will help your team think of many possible ideas. You might take some time to **brainstorm** a list of ideas before you decide exactly how to do the task or solve the problem. By brainstorming, your team might come up with better ideas. Then you will not waste time or supplies.

These ideas will help your team brainstorm many ideas before selecting the one you want to use:

- State any idea that comes to your mind.

- Record everyone's ideas. Don't judge whether the ideas are good or bad until you finish brainstorming.

- Keep thinking of ideas for at least three to five minutes.

- If you can't think of an idea, look at something already on the list. Try to add something to that idea or give it a new twist.

2. **Ask questions to help you understand someone else's ideas.** Most people do not share exactly the same ideas. We all think a little bit differently about what we learn and what we know. This skill will help you communicate better with your teammates. You will learn to express your own ideas more clearly and you will learn different ways to think about an idea or a problem from your teammates.

Whenever you listen to someone else talk, it is easy to misunderstand what that person is trying to say. The person might not communicate very clearly, or you might not hear an important part of the statement or explanation. Before you disagree with another person, ask a question or two to make sure you understand what the person meant to say. If you get a little more information, you might understand her or his idea a lot better. You might even decide that the new idea makes a lot of sense! You might ask questions such as these:

- "I don't understand what you mean. Can you give me an example?"

- "Can you show me what you mean?"

- "Why do you think that? What are your reasons?"

- "I'm not sure I get what you mean. Could you please tell me again?"

Don't automatically say "I don't agree" until you have asked at least one question to help you understand what your teammate is thinking. It's all right to disagree with your teammates' ideas. Just make sure you understand exactly what your teammates mean before you disagree.

3. Criticize ideas, not people. Has anyone ever made fun of you or said something unkind because of something you said? When that happened, how did you feel about yourself and about the other person? Sometimes people have different opinions or ideas, or they want to do things differently. That is the beauty of teamwork. You can share many ideas and learn something in a way you never could have thought of by yourself. If you don't agree with a teammate's idea, you can say you disagree and then give your idea. You can say, "That's one idea. Here is another idea."

Sometimes when people disagree, they say unkind things about the person who said the idea, like, "Do you really think that? You must be pretty stupid." When you disagree with a teammate, tell him or her what you disagree with rather than calling your teammate names. Disagreeing with ideas is helpful for your team because it will make you think through your ideas more clearly. You will probably feel more like offering your own ideas if you know that others won't call you names or put you down.

Team Jobs

The team job descriptions will help you remember what to do when it is your turn to do each job. There is a special colored wristband to wear for each job.

The **materials manager** gets the supplies that are listed under the heading "Team Supplies." When the team finishes the team task, everyone helps clean up the work area. Then the materials manager returns the supplies to the supply table.

The **tracker** keeps track of what the team is doing. The tracker makes sure that the team does every step and follows the directions in order. The tracker might point to each step as the team works on it. If the team needs to stop, the tracker might write the number of the step where the team stopped. Everyone on the team needs to help read and follow the directions. The tracker is not the team's only reader.

If the team gets stuck, the **messenger** may ask another team's messenger for help. Or the messenger may ask your teacher for help. Only the messenger can leave the team and ask for help, though. Everyone else should stay with the team.

The **skill builder** encourages teammates to practice the team skills. The skill builder tells teammates when they are doing the skill well and reminds teammates to listen to one another and to be polite and courteous. The skill builder helps teammates work together and complete the team task.

Doing Science with C.Q. and I.O.

C.Q. and I.O. are characters in your student guide. C.Q. is curious and asks a lot of questions. That is how he got his name. I.O. got her name because she likes to investigate things and observe carefully.

C.Q. and I.O. like to work together to find answers to their questions. Sometimes they will give you some questions to investigate or some problems to solve. They invite you to become curious and questioning too. Look for C.Q. and I.O. for helpful hints and reminders!

Making and Using a Science Notebook

Scientists document what they do by writing, drawing, and making charts and graphs. They call what they write or draw a record. When you do science, you need to keep records of what you do too. Most of the time, you will keep your records in a science notebook.

A science notebook is like a diary. In it, you keep all your records about what happens in an investigation. What you write in a notebook also helps you remember what you did, how you did it, what you observed, when something happened, and what you learned. The icon of the notebook will help you remember when to record something, but you can use your notebook at other times too.

Each time you check on an investigation, you should record in your notebook. You can draw pictures, take measurements, and write descriptions of what you observed or how you did something. You can add special pages like calendar pages or handouts to your notebook. The more information you record in your notebook, the easier it will be to describe what happened during your investigation. Your records will also help you explain why you think something happened.

In your notebook, you can keep track of questions you wonder about. Then you can design your own investigations to find the answers to your questions.

Doing Science Safely

Doing science is interesting and a lot of fun. But just like scientists, you might sometimes work with equipment and materials that could cause harm to you or your clothing. When you see the caution hand, pay special attention to the safety hints. Remember to always handle your materials and equipment exactly as the directions say you should. Even common, everyday items can be hazardous when not handled carefully!

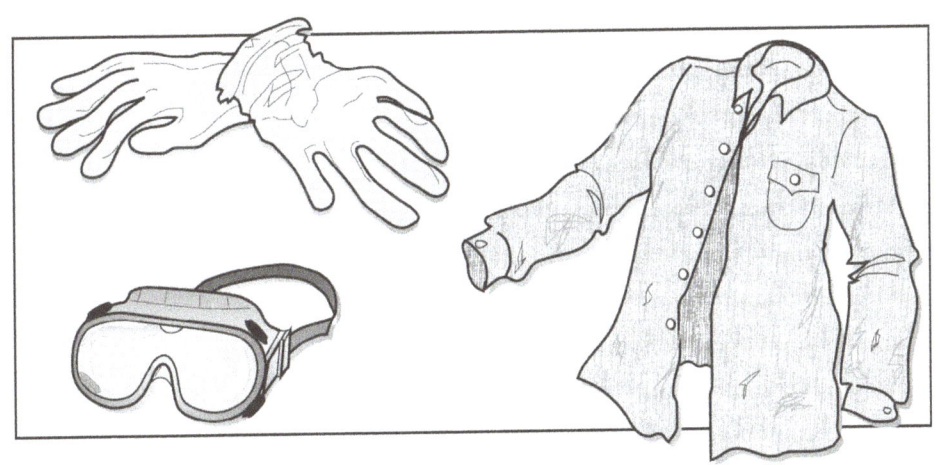

Previewing the Student Guide

Take a tour of your guide with your teacher.

1. Locate the table of contents. How is a table of contents helpful?

2. Locate the glossary. How is a glossary helpful?

3. Select a lesson.

    a. Look through the lesson looking for titles, headings, and subheadings. What clues do the text sizes give you about the lesson?

    b. Locate the "Team Task," "Team Skills," "Team Jobs," "Team Supplies," and "Directions" sections. How are these things organized to help you learn?

    c. Look for visual clues (photographs, illustrations, charts, graphs, and icons). How can these clues help you learn?

    d. Look for boldfaced words. Why would some words be boldfaced?

4. Look through another lesson. How are the lessons similar? How are they different?

5. How can this guide help you learn? How can it help you think like a scientist?

Digging In!

You have learned a little about doing science. You have begun to think about what it means to do science. You have reviewed the importance of working as a team. You have talked about team skills and special team skills. You have looked at team job descriptions. You know that C.Q. and I.O. are eager helpers. You have made your science notebook. You know what sign to look for to make sure that you work safely. You have also previewed the text to understand how it is organized to help you learn. Now it is time to put on your scientist cap and begin doing science!

Lesson 1

Believe It or Not

Would you believe this ad if you read it in a magazine, comic book, or newspaper? Why or why not?

Do You Believe the Ad?

Sharing Ideas

After you read what Heidi and Carlos have to say about Muscle Powder, answer these questions in your notebook. Share your answers with your classmates.

1. What is Carlos's main point?

2. What is Heidi's main point?

3. What do you think of the points they are making?

4. Why do you think people want to believe ads that promise quick and easy methods for self-improvement?

5. How would you investigate whether Muscle Powder works?

6. Where would you get evidence to use in your investigation?

Look at the Evidence

When scientists investigate questions, they use their senses, take measurements, make observations, and record their evidence. You can use the same processes to collect **direct evidence**.

Sometimes, though, it is useful to collect evidence by finding out what someone else has observed or measured. This type of evidence is called **indirect evidence**. You don't collect evidence directly yourself, but rely on the evidence collected by others.

The trick about using indirect evidence is that you must consider the quality of the evidence carefully. Just because something is written in a magazine, published on the World Wide Web, or stated by an adult does not mean it is true. The following questions might help you decide if you should pay attention to the indirect evidence you are reading or hearing:

- Who is the person making the claim?

- Is the person qualified in some way to make the claim? For example, does the person have special training, education, or experience that qualifies him or her as an expert in that area?

A **claim** is a statement that someone wants you to think is true.

- What direct evidence does the person state to support his or her claim?

- Did the person investigate the claim directly?

- Who will benefit if people use the product or service?

- Did the claim make sense to you?

- Is there a way to test the claim?

These questions can help you review someone else's claims with scientific **skepticism**. If you are skeptical, you do not believe everything you read or hear without questioning it. Remember that even the experts don't always agree.

Would You Be Taken In?

Many magazines, newspapers, and television commercials advertise products that promise to improve a person's body or appearance in some way. Some of the products are worthwhile and some are not. Can you tell the difference?

■ Team Task

Analyze the claims made in an advertisement about a fitness product or service. Decide whether your team believes the ad and explain why or why not.

■ Team Jobs

Tracker

Messenger

Skill Builder

■ Team Skills

Move into your team quickly and quietly.

Stay with your team.

Speak softly.

Share and take turns.

Do your job.

Team Supplies

- each teammate's notebook
- 3 pencils
- 3 wristbands

Directions

1. Read the ad for Muscle Powder on page 23.

   a. Find at least two claims you want to know more about.

   b. Write these claims in your notebook.

2. For each claim you and your teammates find in the ad for Muscle Powder, identify these things.

   a. What direct evidence is given to support the claim?

   b. What indirect evidence is given to support the claim?

Engage

3. Discuss with your teammates whether the claims are believable or not.

Planning Ahead

Find an advertisement that promises to change a person's body. Look in comic books, magazines, or newspapers for these ads. Bring one or more ads to class. Check with an adult before you cut out the ad. Bring in the magazine if you cannot cut out the ad.

Becoming a Skeptical Scientist

Muscle Powder is a make-believe product, but there are many products you can buy that are a lot like Muscle Powder. How can you tell whether an ad sells a product that is helpful or harmful?

Team Task

Identify the claims in a real advertisement. Then make a list of evidence offered in the ad that supports the claims. Decide if the ad is believable and explain your reasons.

Team Jobs

Tracker

Messenger

Skill Builder

Team Skills

Discuss many ideas before selecting one.

Team Supplies

- advertisements for body improvement
- each teammate's notebook
- 3 pencils
- 3 wristbands

Directions

1. Number or name each ad.

2. In your notebook, make a data table with six columns, like this one.

Name of fitness ad	Source of ad	Target audience	Claims	Do you believe the claims?	Why or why not?

3. Complete all six columns in the data table for each ad.

4. Decide which ad your team will share with the class and prepare a short presentation.

   a. Review the questions in "Sharing Ideas."

   b. Decide who will do which parts of the presentation.

> Be sure every team member has a part in the presentation.

Sharing Ideas

As you share the fitness ad your team selected, be sure to include information that answers these questions.

1. What message does this ad send the reader about fitness?

2. What message does this ad send the reader about ideal bodies?

3. Who is the target audience for this product or service? Why do you think the advertisers are selling to that audience?

Deepen Understanding through Vocabulary

1. Complete a "Verbal and Visual Word Association Chart" for the terms evidence and skepticism. Look through your notebook and text for ideas.

2. Be prepared to share your chart with the class.

✓ Checking Understanding

Part A: Talk about the following questions with your teammates. Then write your own response to each question in your notebook.

1. Is it important to be skeptical and look for evidence when reading or listening to ads? Why or why not?

2. Is it important for scientists to be skeptical? Why or why not?

3. Is it important for scientists to base their claims on evidence? Why or why not?

Part B: Review the "Doing Science" section on pages 1–9. Look at the graphic organizer on page 2. Talk about ways that you were doing science during this lesson. Then, on your own, describe ways in which you were doing science in your notebook.

Part C: Think about the activities that you did and the strategies that you used during this lesson. Talk about the following questions with your teammates. Then write your own response to each question in your notebook.

1. What did you learn during this lesson?

2. What activities or strategies helped you learn? How or why were they helpful?

3. Did working as a team help you learn? Why or why not?

4. What skills did your team do well? What skills does your team need to improve?

Lesson 2

Muscles, Bones, and Fitness

What kinds of activities do you like to do? How many of them involve using your muscles and bones?

Your Bones and Muscles

Your Skeleton

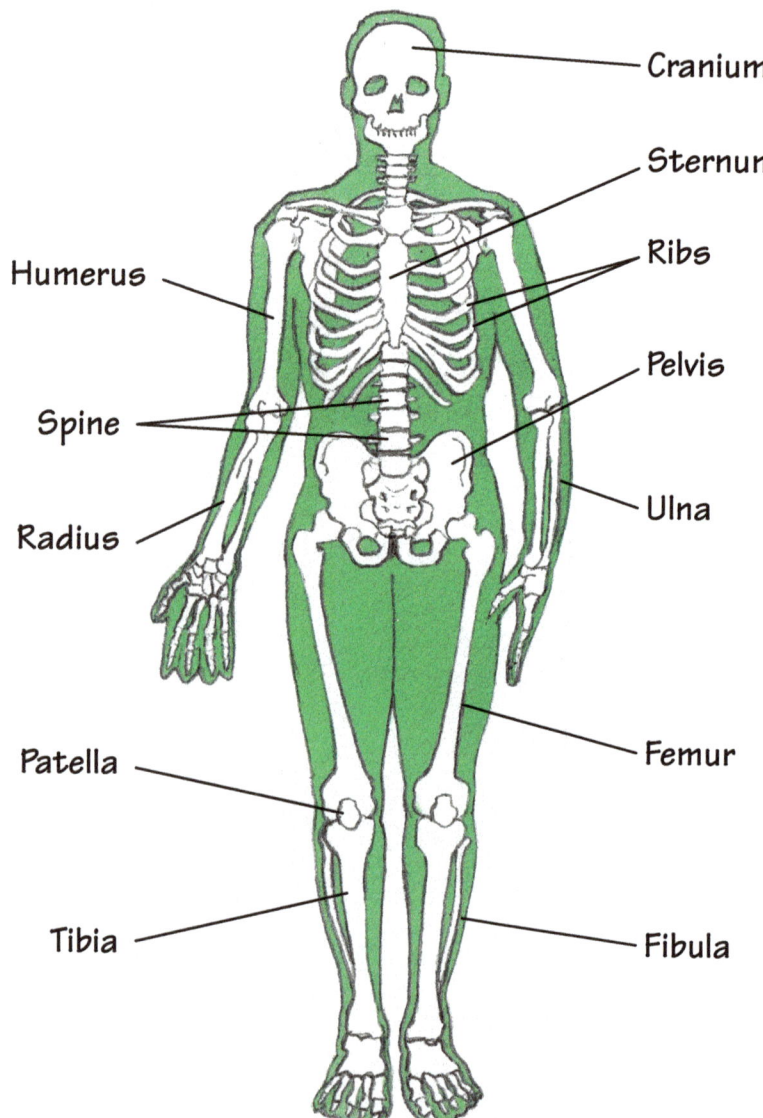

The bones of your **skeleton** have three main functions: support, protection, and movement. First, bones support every part of your body. They make the strong framework that allows you to stand. Second, they protect soft organs by enclosing them. For example, the skull encloses and protects your brain, and the rib cage encloses and protects your heart and lungs. Third, bones allow your body to move.

When you were born, you started with about 350 soft bones. As you grew, your bones began to grow together. By the time you will be in your midtwenties, your body will have about 206 individual bones. The diagram illustrates some of the major bones in your body. Do you recognize any of the names?

Your Muscles

Forty to 50 percent of your body weight is made of muscle. You have three types of muscle: **skeletal muscle**, **smooth muscle**, and **cardiac muscle**.

1. The type of muscle attached to your bones is called skeletal muscle. Skeletal muscles are the ones that allow you to move and be active. Skeletal muscles are the ones you can make stronger with exercise. You can control this kind of muscle and decide when to move it.

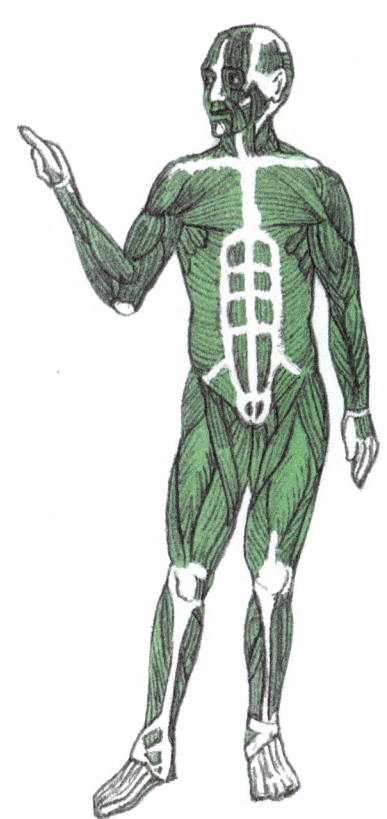

Explore-Explain

2. Smooth muscles are those found in organs such as your diaphragm, lungs, blood vessels, and stomach. Smooth muscles operate automatically all the time. You don't have to think to make your smooth muscles work. Your brain sends signals to them constantly so that they keep on working. For example, you don't decide to take a breath each time you breathe; your lungs and diaphragm move without your thinking about them.

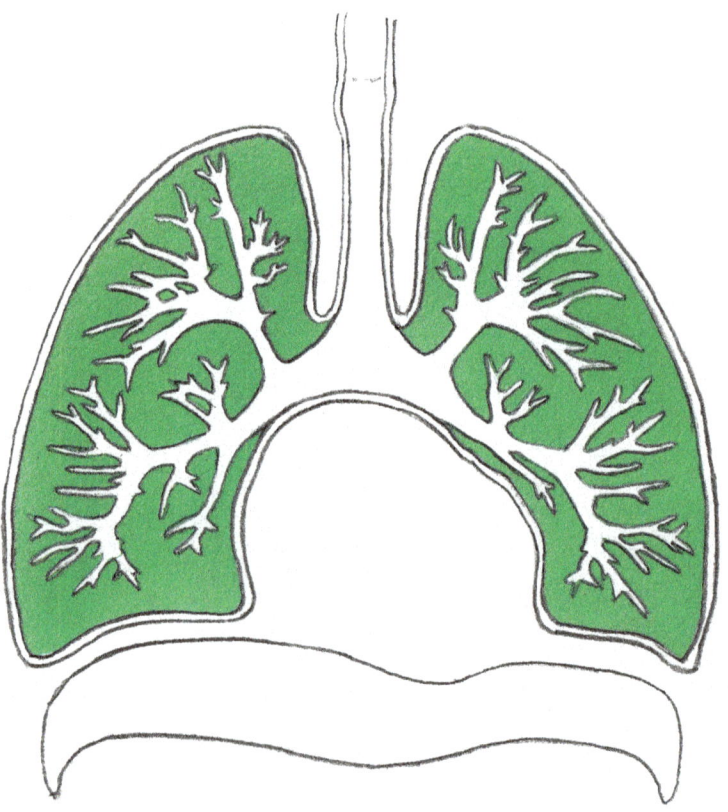

3. Cardiac muscle is found only in the heart. Cardiac muscle is extremely strong and works all the time. Luckily, you don't have to think about making your heart beat many times each minute!

Your bones and your muscles working together are called the **musculoskeletal system**. The musculoskeletal system is your body's system for movement.

Exploring Muscles

What are muscles and how do they work? Can you make your muscles stronger?

▮ *Team Task*

After each member of the team learns something about muscles in an "expert" group, share with one another what each member has learned. Complete three activities that will help you learn about your muscles.

▮ *Team Jobs*

Materials Manager   Tracker   Messenger

▮ *Team Skills*

Ask questions to help you understand someone else's ideas.

▮ *Team Supplies*

- 1 plastic tray
- each teammate's notebook
- 3 pencils
- 3 wristbands

Supplies for Materials Managers

- 1 paper fastener
- 1 pair of scissors
- 2 narrow pieces of cardboard, each 20 centimeters long
- 2 pieces of string, each about 20 centimeters long
- 1 copy of "Muscles and Bones: Study Sheet for Materials Managers"

Supplies for Trackers

- 1 bathroom scale (to be shared by teams)
- 1 copy of "Strengthening Your Muscles: Study Sheet for Trackers"

Supplies for Messengers

- 1 clip clothespin
- 1 watch or clock with a second hand
- 1 copy of "Muscle Endurance: Study Sheet for Messengers"

Directions

1. Collect and distribute the supplies to each team member.

> Materials managers from all teams will form an expert group; trackers, a second group; and messengers, a third group.

2. Join your expert group.

   a. Read the information on the study sheet with your expert team members.

   b. Complete the activity described on your study sheet.

   c. Review the information so that you can share it with your teammates.

3. Return to your team.

   a. One at a time, share the information from your expert group.

   b. Make sure that everyone understands the information.

4. As a team, discuss answers to the questions in "Ideas to Think About." Write answers in your own notebook.

46   Lesson 2: Muscles, Bones, and Fitness

Ideas to Think About

Read and discuss the following questions with your teammates. Then write your own response to each question in your notebook.

1. What is the purpose of your bones and muscles?

2. Describe how you think skeletal muscles work.

3. What can you do to make your muscles strong?

4. What can you do to increase your endurance?

Steroids: Muscle Madness

"Muscle" drugs, known as **steroids**, have shaken up the sports world. A number of top sports competitors lost their medals when evidence of steroids showed up in their urine tests. Increased use of steroids by young people has caused even more worry.

Steroid users hope these artificial hormones will quickly increase their muscle size and weight, but the drugs have some scary side-effects. Female users may develop beards or stop their menstrual periods. Males may become overly aggressive or develop breasts. Steroid use can lead to serious liver problems. If taken before reaching full height, steroids can stunt a person's growth.

Users who take steroids without medical advice may know little about the side effects. They see the drugs as an aid to winning a place on the school team. They don't realize the serious risks they're taking. But the experts agree—steroids and sports don't mix. There are no short cuts to becoming a trained athlete.

Sharing Ideas

Talk about these questions with your classmates.

1. Why do you think people try dangerous drugs like steroids to build muscle strength?

2. How might you get stronger and better at a sport or activity without taking steroids?

3. What are the special dangers of steroids for kids?

4. If you suspect that a friend might be thinking about taking steroids, how would you convince him or her not to take steroids?

Time to Move

The key to having strong muscles is to keep your body active. Doing exercises is one way to keep active and get in shape! Choose one exercise in each of the sets of exercises from the "Exercise Appendix" on pages 149–165. Then try them.

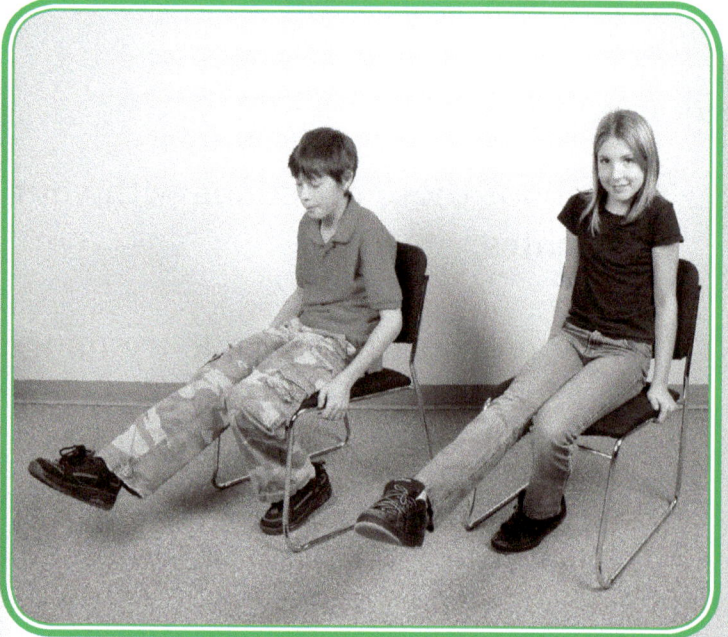

1. After each exercise, record how your body responded.

2. Do all the exercises have the same effect on your body? Compare the exercises according to these questions.

   a. Which exercises stretched your muscles?

   b. Which exercises tired your muscles?

   c. Which exercises made you breathe hard?

   d. Which exercises made your heart beat fast?

   e. Which exercises helped you relax some part of your body?

3. Which exercises would you do again?

✓ Checking Understanding

Part A: Talk about the following questions with your teammates. Then write your own response to each question in your notebook.

1. Describe the musculoskeletal system.

2. What is the purpose of the musculoskeletal system?

3. What can you do to keep your muscles strong?

Part B: Review the "Doing Science" section on pages 1–9. Look at the graphic organizer on page 2. Talk about ways that you were doing science during this lesson. Then, on your own, describe ways in which you were doing science in your notebook.

Part C: Think about the activities that you did and the strategies that you used during this lesson. Talk about the following questions with your teammates. Then write your own response to each question in your notebook.

1. What did you learn during this lesson?

2. What activities or strategies helped you learn? How or why were they helpful?

3. Did working as a team help you learn? Why or why not?

4. What skills did your team do well? What skills does your team need to improve?

Lesson 3

Count the Beats

In lesson 2, you observed how your body responded to different exercises. Some of your observations related to what your heart was doing. In lesson 3, you will learn more about your heart. You will compare your heart rate at rest, during exercise, and after exercise. You will explore what happens to your heart during exercise. You will also understand why exercising your heart is important to overall physical fitness.

Your Cardiovascular System

Your heart pounds during and after you exercise because you have used your **cardiovascular system**. The cardiovascular system consists of the heart, arteries, veins, capillaries, and blood. It carries nutrients, energy in the form of sugar, and oxygen around to the cells of your body. Cells are the small units that make up your muscles, organs, bones, and everything else in your body.

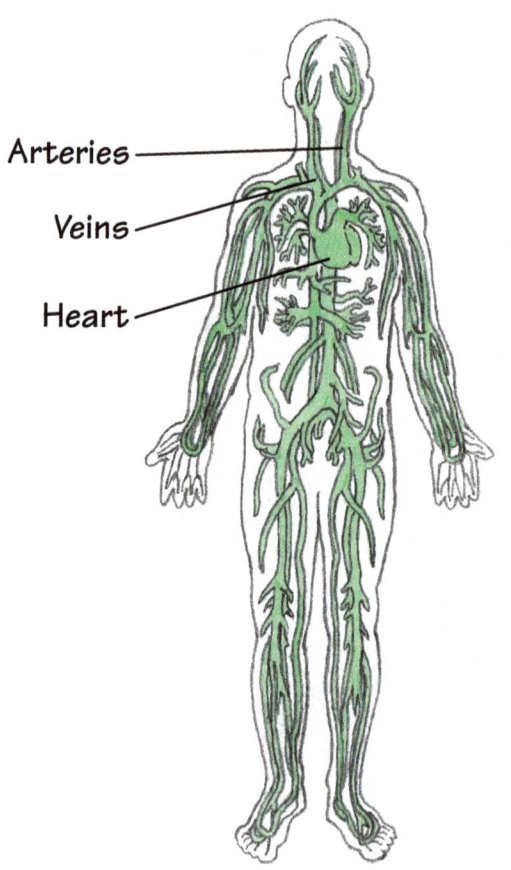

Your Blood Vessels

To transport all these materials around the body, the blood needs to be pumped. The heart is your body's pump. The blood vessels provide the tubing for the blood to move around the body. There are three types of blood vessels: **arteries**, **veins**, and **capillaries**. Arteries are thick and muscular and carry blood away from the heart. Veins are thinner than arteries and carry blood back to the heart. Capillaries are the tiniest vessels and connect the larger arteries and veins. Capillaries are only one cell wide, so they allow the oxygen, carbon dioxide, nutrients, sugar molecules, and other substances to move to and from the blood and into and out of other systems of the body, as needed.

Your Heart

Your heart is an organ made of muscle tissue. The job of your heart muscle is to pump blood throughout your body. The design of the heart makes it an effective pump. The heart is basically hollow, with four compartments surrounded by thick muscle. The two compartments on top are each called an **atrium**. An atrium holds blood coming into the heart. The bottom compartments of the heart are called **ventricles**. The ventricles have thick, muscular walls that push together to pump the blood out of the heart to the rest of the body

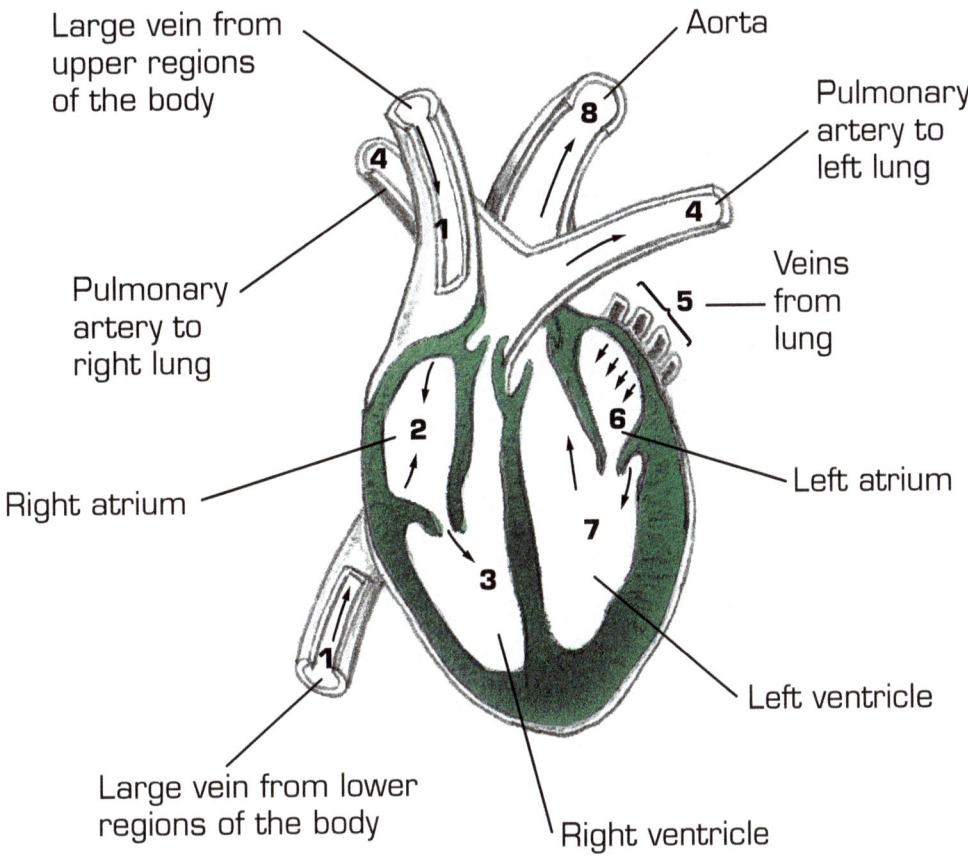

Blood flows into the heart from all over the body (1). First the blood enters the right atrium (2). Then the blood flows into the right ventricle (3) and is pumped to the lungs (4).

Through tiny capillaries, the blood gets oxygen from the air sacs in the lungs. The blood also gets rid of carbon dioxide. The blood that is full of oxygen flows from the lungs (5) into the left atrium of the heart (6). Then the blood flows into the left ventricle (7) and is pumped out to the body through the aorta (8).

Explore-Explain

Just like other muscles in your body, your heart becomes stronger when you exercise it. Aerobic activities, like fast walking, running, playing soccer, and swimming, help exercise your heart.

Finding Your Pulse

You have cardiac muscle in only one place in your body—your heart. In lesson 2, you learned that cardiac muscle is very strong. Your heart beats all the time, even when you are sleeping. Does your heart ever change how hard or how fast it beats? Let's find out!

To answer these questions, you need to know how to measure your **heart rate**—how fast your heart beats in one minute. You can do this by finding and measuring your **pulse**. Here's how it works.

When the heart muscle squeezes, it pushes the blood hard enough for you to feel it in the arteries that are near the surface of your skin. This "push" of the blood against the walls of your arteries is your pulse. One place where you can feel your pulse easily is at your wrist just above your thumb.

To find the pulse in your wrist, turn one hand so your palm faces up. Place the flat part of two fingers of your other hand against the thumb side of your wrist. Press firmly, feeling between the two bones in that part of your arm. (Don't use your thumb to feel your pulse, because your thumb has a pulse of its own.)

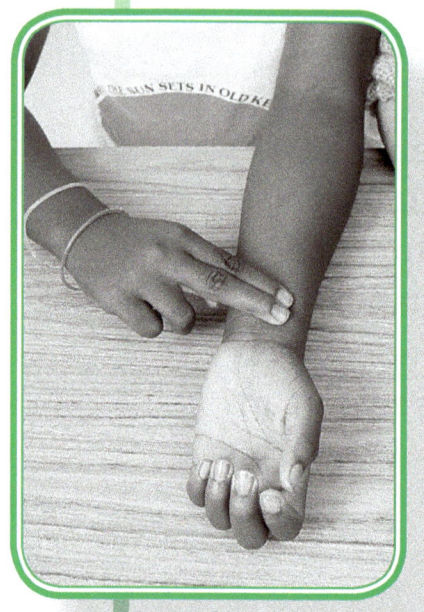

To measure your heart rate, keep your fingers pressed against your wrist. Count the number of times you feel the blood pulse, or push, through your artery in 60 seconds (one minute). Count the first pulse as zero.

On Your Own

Measuring Your Heart Rate

How fast does your heart beat, on average, when you are resting? Does it change when you exercise? What do you think will happen when you measure your heart rate before, during, and after exercise?

Your Task

Collect and record data about your heart rate at rest, during exercise, and after exercise. Then analyze the data to find a relationship between your heart rate and exercise.

Your Supplies

- your notebook
- 1 pencil
- 1 clock with a second hand

Directions

How many times should you measure your heart rate to find the average?

1. As a class, decide how you should conduct this investigation. Review the task. Talk about how you can collect and record data about your average heart rate at rest, during exercise, and after exercise.

2. In your notebook, make a data table in which to record your data.

3. Before you exercise, predict whether your heart rate (pulse rate) will change when you exercise. Write your prediction and an explanation for it in your notebook.

Remember that every time your heart squeezes, or "beats", you feel your pulse (pulse rate = heart rate).

A prediction is a scientist's way of describing what she or he thinks will happen in an investigation based on what she or he already knows. A prediction is different from a guess because you can explain why you made a prediction. A prediction is based on what you already know. You might write your notebook entry like this: "I predict that my heart rate will not change when I exercise. I think this because I am in good shape."

Lesson 3: Count the Beats

4. Complete your investigation by measuring and recording your heart rate before, during, and after exercise.

5. Using the data in your data table, answer these questions. Write your answers in your notebook.

   a. Did your heart rate change? If so, explain how it changed before, during, and after exercise.

   b. Did your heart rate return to its resting rate after exercise? If so, how long did it take?

   c. Do you think the cardiac muscle in your heart can get stronger through exercise, as the other muscles in your body can? Explain your answer.

6. Record your average heart rates on the class charts.

Making Bar Graphs of the Class Data

You and your classmates each recorded three heart rates on your class charts. You recorded your average heart rate at rest, during exercise, and after exercise. To make sense of those numbers, it is helpful to organize the data in a form that lets you look at all the information at one time. Graphs are one way to organize information. In this activity, your team will create bar graphs to organize the class data.

Team Task

Construct three bar graphs of the class data and compare average heart rates before, during, and after exercise.

Team Jobs

Tracker

Messenger

Skill Builder

Team Skills

Discuss many ideas before selecting one.

Team Supplies

- 1 plastic tray
- 3 rulers
- 3 sheets of graph paper
- each teammate's notebook
- colored pencils or markers (optional)
- 3 pencils
- 3 wristbands

Directions

1. Review "How to Make a Bar Graph" on pages 68–69.

2. Talk about how you will make a bar graph of the class data of heart rates at rest. Use these questions to help you.

    a. How will you label the horizontal and vertical axes?

    b. What numbers belong on each scale?

    c. How will you make your graph attractive and easy to read?

    d. Which teammate will do which task?

3. Make your graph.

4. Review the graph. Does everyone agree with the results?

   a. If so, sign your name on the graph of resting heart rates.

   b. If not, decide how to correct the graph and make the corrections.

5. Repeat steps 2 through 4 and make bar graphs of the class data for heart rates during and after exercise.

How to Make a Bar Graph

A. Review the data from the class charts.

In what order are the data presented? The average heart rate data on the class charts might not be organized very well. How could you put the class data in order? Do some students report the same average heart rate as other students? How might you group those data?

Note: The term **data** is plural for the word **datum**. One average heart rate is a datum—one piece of data, but we refer to two or more numbers as data. That is why the sentences above say "the data are," and not "the data is."

B. Draw the horizontal axis and vertical axis for the graph. Using graph paper and a ruler will help you keep the lines straight and the bars evenly spaced.

C. Label each axis, using the headings from the class charts. Label the horizontal axis, Average Heart Rate at Rest, and the vertical axis, Number of Students.

D. Decide on the number scales for each axis. You need to leave enough space on both axes for all the numbers that are in the data table. (The word **axes** is the plural of axis.)

Ideas to Think About

Using the information in your graphs, discuss these questions with your teammates. Write your responses in your notebook.

1. How are the graphs similar?

2. How are the graphs different?

3. What was the most common resting heart rate?

4. What was the most common heart rate during exercise and after exercise?

5. Why do you think the most common heart rates on the three graphs are not the same?

6. What do your graphs tell you about the relationship between heart rate and exercise?

What the Heart Does during Exercise

When you exercise, your heart pumps blood to the body so that your muscles receive oxygen. Oxygen acts like a fuel to help your muscles move. When you do **aerobic exercise** regularly, your heart gets stronger and more efficient at pushing blood out to the body so that your muscles get the oxygen they need to keep moving.

The word "aerobic" means "with oxygen." Aerobic exercise is any activity that requires the body to use oxygen for an extended period of time, usually at least 15 to 20 minutes.

Aerobic activities exercise your heart and lungs and help your body circulate oxygen to all your muscles and organs more efficiently. Aerobic activities also help you build **endurance**. Endurance is the ability to do something for a long time.

Your body also can perform **anaerobic** activities. "Anaerobic" means "without oxygen." Sprinting—running very fast for a short period of time—is an anaerobic exercise because your body does not need extra oxygen for short bursts of activity. However, if you want to continue running, swimming, or biking, for example, your muscles need more oxygen. Then the activity becomes aerobic because your muscles need oxygen to continue. No one can do anaerobic activities for very long.

Time to Move Again

As a class, choose a set of aerobic exercises that will exercise your heart and lungs. You can choose exercises or activities from the "Exercise Appendix" on pages 149–165 or suggest some of your own. Remember to include exercises that help your muscles and heart warm up before you do the aerobic activities. Do some "cool-down" (stretching) exercises after you are finished.

As you exercise, pay attention to how your body feels. Is your heart beating faster? Are you breathing harder? Are your muscles getting tired? Try to exercise for at least 15 minutes while your heart rate is faster. That will help your heart become stronger.

✓ Checking Understanding

Part A: Talk about the following questions with your teammates. Then write your own response to each question in your notebook.

1. Describe how you think exercise improves the heart and a person's overall physical fitness.

2. List at least three aerobic activities that you like to do. (An aerobic activity is anything that makes your heart beat faster and makes you breathe harder, like running, swimming, bicycling, dancing, or soccer.)

Part B: Review the "Doing Science" section on pages 1–9. Look at the graphic organizer on page 2. Talk about ways that you were doing science during this lesson. Then, on your own, describe ways in which you were doing science in your notebook.

Part C: Think about the activities that you did and the strategies that you used during this lesson. Talk about the following questions with your teammates. Then write your own response to each question in your notebook.

1. What did you learn during this lesson?

2. What activities or strategies helped you learn? How or why were they helpful?

3. Did working as a team help you learn? Why or why not?

4. What skills did your team do well? What skills does your team need to improve?

Lesson 4

A Breathing System

In the last lesson, you found out that your heart beats faster after you exercise. What happens to your breathing rate when you exercise? What do your lungs do for your body when you breathe?

Your Respiratory System

You probably know that you use your lungs to breathe. You breathe in (**inhale**) and breathe out (**exhale**) many times a day. But why do you breathe in and out? What do inhaling and exhaling have to do with the health of your body? Are your lungs the only parts of your body involved in breathing?

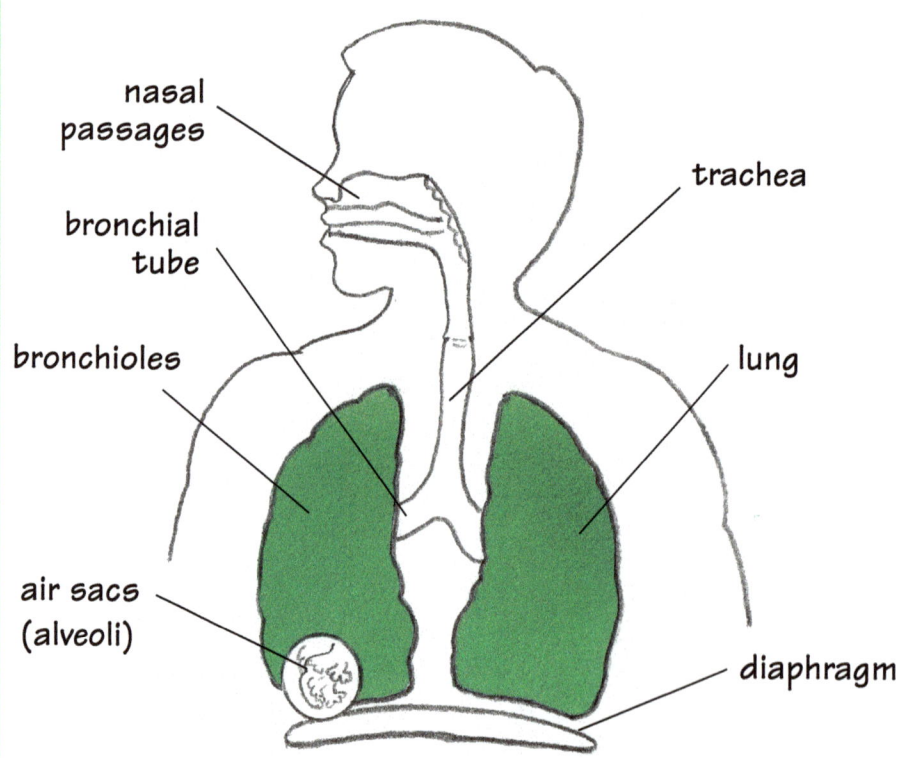

Inhaling

The drawing shows the **respiratory system**. The following steps tell how oxygen in the air travels from outside the body to the cells inside the body.

1. When a person breathes in, air enters the **nasal passages**.

2. Air travels through the throat to the **trachea**.

3. The trachea divides into two tubes called **bronchial tubes**.

4. The bronchial tubes lead to the **lungs**.

5. In the lungs, the bronchial tubes divide many times into smaller branches called **bronchioles**.

6. At the end of the tiny branches are **air sacs**. It is here that oxygen in the air passes to the blood that is inside the capillaries. The blood carries the oxygen to the heart, which then pumps the blood with oxygen around the body.

7. The **diaphragm** is a thick sheet of smooth muscle at the bottom of the chest cavity. It moves down when a person inhales. It moves up when a person exhales.

When you exercise or do an activity that requires extra energy, your muscles need more oxygen than usual. As a result, your respiratory system must work harder and faster to get more oxygen into the blood so that the blood can carry the oxygen to your muscles.

Exhaling

The respiratory system also is important because of what happens when you exhale. Carbon dioxide is a waste product that is made by cells when they turn sugars into energy to keep the cells alive. The cells must get rid of the carbon dioxide, which becomes a poison to the body if the body has too much of it at one time.

When the blood cells absorb oxygen from the air in the air sacs (**alveoli**), they also give up the carbon dioxide waste that the blood cells collected from other body cells. The air that you exhale, therefore, has less oxygen and more carbon dioxide in it than the air you inhaled. (With each breath, you do exhale some oxygen too. That is why people can perform "rescue breathing" as part of CPR—cardiopulmonary resuscitation—to help someone who has stopped breathing. If your breath had no oxygen at all, you couldn't help another person breathe.)

Making a Model of the Respiratory System

You have read about the respiratory system. You have read about the parts of the respiratory system. Do you really understand how the respiratory system works? How can you find out how the parts of the system interact? After all, it would be difficult to observe your own respiratory system or the respiratory systems of your classmates.

What can you do if you want to investigate a system that you cannot observe? One way you can investigate a system is to make a **model** of it. Then you can study the model to learn about the real system. In this activity, your team will make a model of the respiratory system.

■ Team Task

Make a model of the respiratory system. Demonstrate and describe how the parts interact.

■ Team Jobs

Materials Manager Tracker Messenger

Lesson 4: A Breathing System

Team Skills

Ask questions to help you understand someone else's ideas.

Team Supplies

- 1 plastic tray
- 1 plastic straw
- 1 clear plastic cup with a hole in the bottom
- 1 small balloon
- 1 large balloon
- 1 pair of scissors
- masking tape
- each teammate's notebook
- 3 pencils
- 3 wristbands

Directions

1. Stretch the small balloon with your hands. Each teammate should do this.

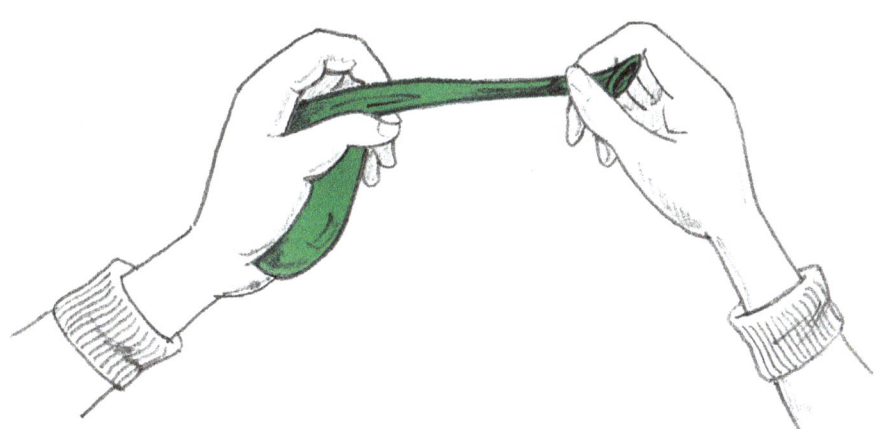

Explore-Explain 83

2. Put the small balloon over one end of the straw.

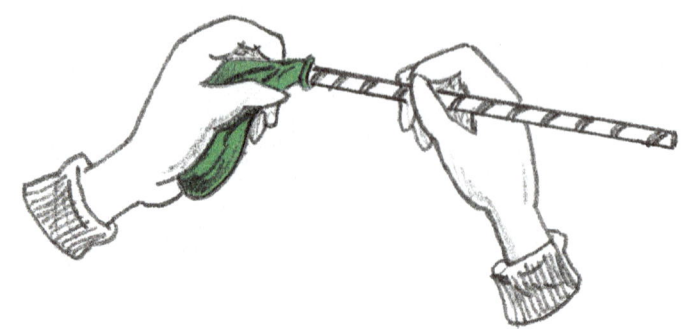

3. Tape the balloon tightly to the straw.

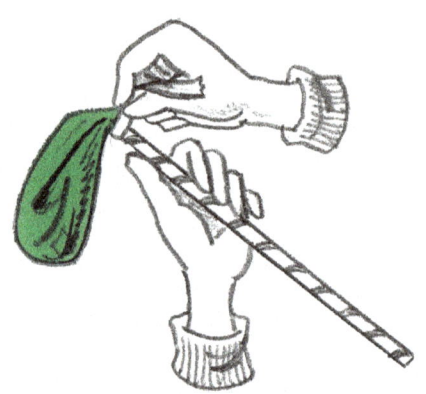

Be sure everyone gets a turn to do something while you are making the model.

4. Turn the cup upside down and put the straw through the hole in the bottom of the cup so that the balloon is inside the cup.

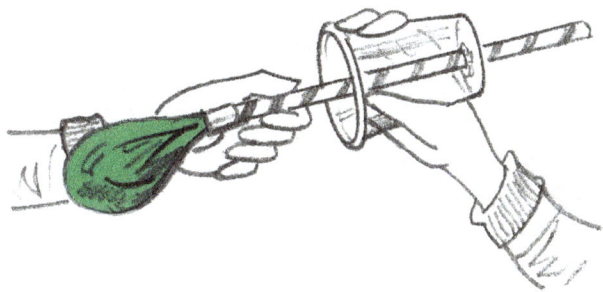

5. Pull the straw through the hole so that the small balloon hangs inside the plastic cup. Tape the straw to the cup.

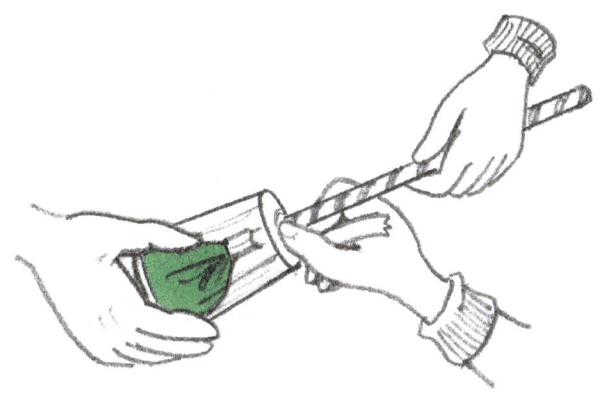

6. Cut the narrow part (the part you blow through) off the large balloon.

7. Stretch out the bottom part of the balloon so that it lies flat.

8. Stretch the piece of rubber from the large balloon over the wide, open part of the cup. Use masking tape to tape this piece of rubber tightly to the cup.

Be sure you tape the piece of rubber tightly so it cannot fall off or be pulled off the cup.

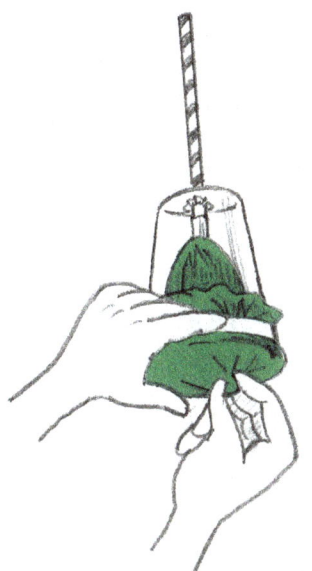

9. Pull on the piece of rubber on the outside of the cup. Observe what happens.

Take turns pulling on the piece of rubber. Share your observations.

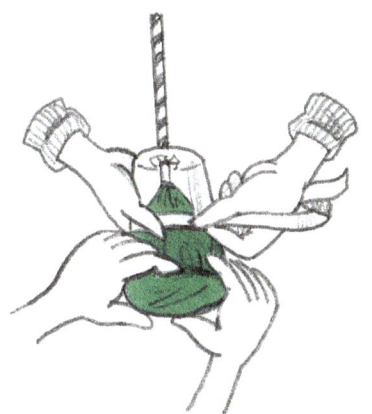

Explore-Explain 87

10. As you observe the model of the respiratory system, relate the model to the diagram of the respiratory system on page 78.

a. Draw a picture of the model in your notebook.

b. Label the parts to match those in the diagram of the respiratory system on page 78.

c. Write a sentence that describes how the model works.

Ideas to Think About

With your team, discuss your ideas about these questions.

1. How is the model like the human respiratory system?

2. How is the model different from the human respiratory system?

3. How does a model help you learn about the "real thing"?

On Your Own

Breathing and Exercise

When you exercised in lesson 3, what happened to your heart rate? What do you think will happen to your breathing rate when you exercise? Do some exercises and find out!

Your Task

Measure and record your breathing rate at rest and then after exercise. Find out how long it takes for your breathing rate to return to its resting rate. Share your data.

Your Supplies

- 1 watch or clock with a second hand
- 1 pencil
- your notebook

Directions

1. Sit still for five minutes. Then count the number of breaths you take in one minute.

   a. Use the clock to time yourself.

   b. Record the number of breaths in your notebook.

   c. Label this number "Resting rate."

2. Now run in place for two minutes.

Breathing in and then out again counts as one breath.

3. Count the number of breaths you take in the first minute after you stop exercising.

   a. Use the clock to time yourself.

   b. Record the number of breaths in your notebook.

   c. Label this number "Exercising rate."

4. Continue to count your breaths each minute until the number of breaths matches your resting rate.

   a. Record the number of breaths after two minutes, three minutes, four minutes, and so on, until your breathing rate matches your resting rate from step 1.

   b. How many minutes did it take for your breathing to return to normal?

As you read this article from *Current Health* magazine, think about how you can take care of your respiratory system and why that is important.

It's Breath-taking! The Respiratory System

Breathing is the first thing you do when you're born and it doesn't stop until you die. You can hold your breath. You can take deep breaths. But most of the time breathing is so automatic you never even think about it. If you do pay attention to your breathing, you may be surprised to learn that you breathe more than 21,000 times every day! ...

Your Air Supply

Did you know that you use about 5,000 gallons of air every day? Most of the air is a gas called nitrogen. About one-fifth of the air you breathe in is oxygen; about one-hundredth is carbon dioxide.

You don't use all the oxygen you take in. Some of it is still in the air you breathe out. The leftover oxygen makes rescue breathing possible. That's why you can help someone who has stopped breathing. You can blow air into the person's mouth and lungs. Rescue breathing is part of CPR. The letters CPR stand for cardiopulmonary resuscitation.

The lungs are more in touch with the outside air than is any other part of the body, even more than the skin. If you could spread out the space in your lungs, it would take up 40 times more space than the area covered by your skin! If 40 students your size stood together, the total amount of space used by everyone's skin would be about the same as the space inside one person's lungs. That's why clean air is so important.

But air has more than nitrogen, oxygen, and carbon dioxide in it. Air is also full of dirt and germs. The dirt and germs can hurt the respiratory system. ...

Sneezes and Wheezes

The lungs are able to protect themselves from dirt and germs in the air. If something blocks or irritates your airways, you can sneeze or cough. The lining of the lungs and the nose traps dirt. Tiny hairs beat back and forth. They send the dirt back to the throat. Sometimes dirt or germs get through to the air spaces. Groups of large white cells eat or remove dirt and germs so they can't hurt you.

The lungs can't keep everything out. That's often why you get sick. Have you ever had a cold or the flu? These illnesses are caused by germs that attack the lungs. ...

Be Good to Your Respiratory System

Other diseases can hurt the respiratory system. Some make breathing hard by blocking airways. Some slow down blood flow in the lungs. Others make it hard for the chest cavity to let in air. Lung cancer is one of the worst diseases of the respiratory system. Anyone who smokes has a chance of getting it. ... You can do a lot to keep your respiratory system healthy. ...

Stay Smoke-Free

The most important way to keep your respiratory system healthy is not to smoke. Cigarette smoke contains at least 200 different poisons. Smoking slows down or stops the movement of hairs that clean the airways. It also slows down blood flow in the lungs. It makes it hard for the blood to carry oxygen.

Smoke from someone else's cigarette, called second-hand smoke, can hurt you even if you never puff on a cigarette. Second-hand smoke has more poison than smoke from a cigarette people smoke themselves. Second-hand smoke has twice as much of the poisons tar and nicotine, and three times as much of the poison carbon monoxide. Children who live in a house with a smoker are twice as likely to get sick as children who live in a smoke-free home. The best advice is: If you don't smoke, don't start. If you do smoke, quit. ... If you eat right, exercise, and never smoke, you'll keep your lungs and the rest of your respiratory system healthy for every breath you take.

✓ Checking Understanding

Part A: Talk about the following questions with your teammates. Then write your own response to each question in your notebook.

1. During exercise, your breathing rate increases and your heart rate increases. What is your explanation for why your body reacts this way when you exercise? Think about these things to help you develop your explanation.

   a. When you breathe, what work is your respiratory system doing?

   b. How might breathing faster help your body when you exercise?

   c. What work does your heart do all the time?

   d. How might a fast heart rate help your body when you exercise?

2. People who exercise often and are very fit do not pant (breathe hard) when they climb a flight of stairs. People who are not in very good shape often have to pant and rest when they climb a flight of stairs. What is your explanation of why this happens?

Part B: Review the "Doing Science" section on pages 1–9. Look at the graphic organizer on page 2. Talk about ways that you were doing science during this lesson. Then, on your own, describe ways in which you were doing science in your notebook.

Part C: Think about the activities that you did and the strategies that you used during this lesson. Talk about the following questions with your teammates. Then write your own response to each question in your notebook.

1. What did you learn during this lesson?

2. What activities or strategies helped you learn? How or why were they helpful?

3. Did working as a team help you learn? Why or why not?

4. What skills did your team do well? What skills does your team need to improve?

Lesson 5

Fitness from the Inside Out

In lessons 2, 3, and 4, you explored the musculoskeletal, cardiovascular, and respiratory systems. Learning about something can lead to more questions. What questions do you have about fitness, your body systems, and how the systems work together? In lesson 5, you will explore how body systems interact.

Sometimes scientists have to research their questions. As you research answers to your questions, you are going to use the processes involved in doing science.

Researching Questions

Sometimes scientists research questions that they have to see if other people have investigated their questions. You are going to do research on a question that you have to see if someone has investigated your question.

■ Team Task

Research the answer to a question you have about exercise and its effects on your body systems.

■ Team Jobs

Materials Manager   Tracker   Messenger

■ Team Skills

Ask questions to help you understand someone else's ideas.

■ Team Supplies

- library resources, access to the World Wide Web, or both
- each teammate's notebook
- 3 pencils
- 3 wristbands

Directions

1. **Ask questions.** Brainstorm a list of questions that you have about your body during and after exercise. The following questions might help you get started.

    a. Why am I breathing so hard?

    b. Why is my heart pounding?

    c. Why are my muscles sore?

2. **Investigate.** Select one question that your team is interested in researching. Remember that you will need to relate your question to the roles of and interactions between the respiratory, cardiovascular, and musculoskeletal systems.

3. **Use tools.** What tools or resources will help you investigate the answer to your question? How can you find out what parts of the body are related to your question? Identify at least three different sources of information.

> You may use your student guide, encyclopedias, the World Wide Web, and any other reference materials.

4. **Keep records**. As you gather information, write notes and draw pictures in your notebook that will help you answer your question. Keep track of where (what resources) you got your information.

5. **Develop an explanation**. When you have gathered enough information, write a complete answer to the question in your notebook. Remember that you will need to relate your question to the roles of and interactions between the respiratory, cardiovascular, and musculoskeletal systems. You can include pictures in your explanation. Make sure that everyone in your team understands and agrees with the explanation.

6. **Share ideas**. Share your question and explanation with the class. Make sure that every teammate has a role in the presentation.

The Human System: How Everything Works Together

Your body is an incredible machine. Under its skin lie hundreds of muscles, bones, blood vessels, and many organs. These and other parts work night and day keeping your body functioning in ways you often take for granted.

Your body is a collection of systems. Each system has one major role, but it works together with other systems to accomplish the complex job of keeping you alive and healthy. How do the systems you read about work together?

When you are running or hiking or bicycling or playing soccer, you know that your muscles get a workout. But did you know that muscles need oxygen to work or exercise? The harder you work your muscles, the more oxygen they need.

By now, you know that to get oxygen to your muscles, your heart and lungs need to go to work. Every time you take a breath, air is drawn into millions of little air sacs in the lungs. These air sacs transfer oxygen into the tiny blood vessels that run through the walls of the sacs. The heart pumps this oxygen-rich blood to the muscles.

As you begin to exercise, your muscles need more oxygen than usual. To supply this extra oxygen, your lungs begin to draw in more air, sending more oxygen into the air sacs for transfer. Your heart also begins to pump faster, sending more blood to the lungs to pick up the oxygen and hurry it to your muscles. So when you feel your heart beating hard and you are panting, you are helping your body get the extra oxygen you need for your muscles to work hard.

The more your heart and lungs work together this way to supply oxygen to working muscles, the better they get at it.

Just as you can strengthen your muscles by working them over and over, so you can strengthen your heart and lungs by doing regular exercise. Exercise that forces your heart and lungs to work hard together over a period of time is called aerobic exercise. Whenever you work out aerobically, you are letting your heart and lungs practice transporting oxygen from the air into the body. With practice, the heart and lungs get more efficient at this transfer and have to work less hard to provide enough oxygen to your muscles. Have you ever noticed that people who are in really good shape don't seem to pant as much as you do when exercising? That is because their bodies are very good at transferring oxygen from the air to their muscles.

Creative Writing Using the RAFT Strategy

RAFT stands for **r**ole of the writer (the role the writer will assume), **a**udience (who will be reading the writing), **f**ormat (how the writing will be presented), and **t**opic (the subject of the writing). RAFTs are usually fun and humorous, but they also need to show what you have learned. So your story should include real information.

1. Use what you have learned about the respiratory, cardiovascular, and musculoskeletal systems to create a RAFT. Your RAFT should demonstrate your understanding of these body systems and how they interact to help someone become fit. Use the following information to create your RAFT.

    a. Role of the writer: Choose the role of the respiratory system, cardiovascular system, or musculoskeletal system of a "couch potato" who is working to become physically fit because of the President's Council on Physical Fitness and Sports.

    b. Audience: You will be writing to the director of the President's Council on Physical Fitness and Sports.

c. Format: You will write a letter.

d. Topic: The letter will be about the process of becoming physically fit (for example, how you cooperated with other systems or the changes you experienced). According to the President's Council on Physical Fitness and Sports, you are physically fit when your heart, lungs, and muscles are strong and your body is firm and flexible. If you have the energy and strength to do everyday activities without getting tired or hurt, and you still have energy left for fun and for emergencies, then you are physically fit.

2. Be prepared to share your RAFT with the class.

✓ Checking Understanding

Part A: Talk about the following questions with your teammates. Then write your own response to each question in your notebook.

1. How does the musculoskeletal system work with the respiratory system?

2. How does the respiratory system work with the cardiovascular system?

3. How does the cardiovascular system work with the musculoskeletal system?

Part B: Review the "Doing Science" section on pages 1–9. Look at the graphic organizer on page 2. Talk about ways that you were doing science during this lesson. Then, on your own, describe ways in which you were doing science in your notebook.

Part C: Think about the activities that you did and the strategies that you used during this lesson. Talk about the following questions with your teammates. Then write your own response to each question in your notebook.

1. What did you learn during this lesson?

2. What activities or strategies helped you learn? How or why were they helpful?

3. Did working as a team help you learn? Why or why not?

4. What skills did your team do well? What skills does your team need to improve?

Lesson 6

Nutrition and Fitness

Have you ever heard the saying, "You are what you eat"? What do you think the saying means? If you are what you eat, are you more likely to be fast foods or fruits and vegetables? Is what you eat important? Is how much you eat important? Lesson 6 might help you answer these questions.

What Is in the Foods You Eat?

Everyone has to eat to stay alive. But we don't all eat the same kind or same amount of food. Are some foods better for you than others? How can you find out?

■ Team Task

Read the "Nutrition Facts" labels from food containers. Choose the two foods that you think are the most healthy and explain your decision.

■ Team Jobs

Tracker

Messenger

Skill Builder

■ Team Skills

Ask questions to help you understand someone else's ideas.

Team Supplies

- 6 or more empty food packages, each with a "Nutrition Facts" label
- 3 copies of "Nutrients in My Food Record Page"
- each teammate's notebook
- 3 pencils
- 3 wristbands

Directions

1. On your "Nutrients in My Food Record Page," write the names of the foods your team will compare.

2. Read each food label and complete your record page by listing the number of calories in a serving and the percentage (%) of daily value listed for each nutrient.

You could complete your record pages independently by passing around the food packages and filling in the blanks on your own.

A **nutrient** is a substance your body needs to stay healthy. There are six classes of nutrients: carbohydrates, fats, protein, water, vitamins, and minerals. You get the calories you need for energy from the carbohydrates, fats, and protein you eat. The other nutrients help your body in various ways, as explained on the charts that follow.

3. Use the information on your record page and the Charts of nutrients" to evaluate how healthy you think these foods are.

   a. Talk about each food and compare the nutrients.

   b. Number the foods in order from most healthy to least healthy.

4. Write in your notebook why your team chose your number one food as the most healthy.

5. Be prepared to share your information with the class.

Chart of Nutrients

Nutrient	Purpose	Sample Sources
Carbohydrates	provide energy for cells to use	bread, rice, pasta, fruit, cereals, beans
Fats	provide energy; used for making parts of cells and hormones; carry some vitamins	butter, oil, fried foods, meat, nuts, egg yolks, whole milk, cheese
Proteins	provide the building materials to make muscles and to heal wounds; provide energy	meat (beef, pork, chicken, fish), beans (some combined with grains), dairy products, eggs, nuts
Water	hydrates all cells	plain water, fruits, and vegetables
Vitamins		
Vitamin A	helps cells grow, especially skin cells; promotes vision; helps the body fight bacterial infections	green and yellow vegetables like spinach, carrots, and broccoli; liver; fruits like cantaloupe and apricots
Vitamin B_1	helps coordination; keeps you from being tired; helps nerve function	whole grains, nuts, peas, pork, macaroni
Vitamin B_2	helps growth; makes skin soft; breaks down fats	eggs, whole grains, broccoli, cheese, almonds, cottage cheese, milk, spinach
Vitamin B_3	prevents headaches; keeps you from getting tired; maintains skin; breaks down fats	yeast, liver, nuts, eggs, milk, whole grains, chicken, turkey, tuna, salmon
Vitamin B_6	helps body fight disease; maintains skin; helps nerves	whole grains, potatoes, fish, chicken and turkey, red meats, seeds, bananas, spinach, broccoli
Vitamin B_{12}	prevents anemia, headaches, and tiredness	liver, meat, fish, milk
Vitamin C	helps cells stick together; protects against infection; maintains the strength of blood vessels; maintains muscles; helps relieve stress	citrus fruits (oranges, grapefruits, limes, lemons), broccoli, cauliflower, tomatoes, green leafy vegetables
Vitamin D	helps body absorb calcium; important for tooth and bone formation	fortified milk, fish oils, eggs, fatty fish like salmon, sunlight
Vitamin E	protects red blood cells; maintains muscles	plant oils, whole grains, margarine, peanuts, oatmeal, asparagus
Minerals		
Calcium	helps in bone and tooth development; helps muscles to move, blood to clot, and nerve transmission	dairy products, dark green vegetables, tofu, fish with edible bones
Iron	helps blood carry oxygen; protects against disease	meats like liver and beef, spinach, peas, legumes, cereals
Potassium	helps the body store water; helps muscles and nerves function	bananas, whole grains, peanut butter, milk, meat, vegetables
Sodium	helps the body maintain water; helps with muscle and nerve function	table salt, soy sauce, processed foods like sauces and soup

On Your Own

Keeping a Balance

You have compared different foods and decided that some foods are healthier than others, but one food by itself isn't really healthy or unhealthy. What matters is the combination of foods you eat each day. Do you eat the right balance of foods each day? Find out in this activity.

■ Your Task

Compare your daily diet with MyPyramid. Find out how your daily diet "stacks up."

■ Your Supplies

- your notebook
- 1 pencil

Directions

1. In your notebook, list all the foods you ate yesterday.

2. Using the following MyPyramid picture, identify the category for each food item that you listed.

A Close Look at MyPyramid For Kids

MyPyramid for Kids reminds you to be physically active every day, or most days, and to make healthy food choices. Every part of the new symbol has a message for you. Can you figure it out?

Be Physically Active Every Day
The person climbing the stairs reminds you to do something active every day, like running, walking the dog, playing, swimming, biking, or climbing lots of stairs.

Eat More From Some Food Groups Than Others
Did you notice that some of the color stripes are wider than others? The different sizes remind you to choose more foods from the food groups with the widest stripes.

Choose Healthier Foods From Each Group
Why are the colored stripes wider at the bottom of the pyramid? Every food group has foods that you should eat more often than others; these foods are at the bottom of the pyramid.

Every Color Every Day
The colors orange, green, red, yellow, blue, and purple represent the five different food groups plus oils. Remember to eat foods from all food groups every day.

Grains	Vegetables	Fruits	oils	Milk	Meat & Beans
orange	green	red	yellow	blue	purple

Make Choices That Are Right for You
MyPyramid.gov is a Web site that will give everyone in the family personal ideas on how to eat better and exercise more.

Take One Step at a Time
You do not need to change overnight what you eat and how you exercise. Just start with one new, good thing, and add a new one every day.

U.S. Department of Agriculture
Food and Nutrition Service
September 2005
FNS-388

USDA is an equal opportunity provider and employer.

teamnutrition.usda.gov

Elaborate

3. Make a chart like the following one. Identify the number of servings of foods in each category that you ate based on your list.

Food Guide Pyramid Category	Total Number of Servings
Bread, Cereal, Rice & Pasta Group (6–11 servings)	
Vegetable Group (3–5 servings)	
Fruit Group (2–4 servings)	
Milk, Yogurt & Cheese Group (2–3 servings)	
Meat, Poultry, Fish, Dry Beans, Eggs & Nuts Group (2–3 servings)	
Fats, Oils & Sweets (use sparingly)	

How many categories did you meet? In which ones were you over or under?

4. Write in your notebook what you need to eat or not eat to get your daily diet in balance with MyPyramid.

Eating and Digestion

Eating is one of life's greatest pleasures. There are many foods and many ways to build a healthy diet and lifestyle. Enjoy the food you like to eat and take action for good health.

Dietary Guidelines for Healthy Eating

The U.S. Department of Agriculture (USDA) provides the latest information for making healthy decisions about what and how much Americans should eat. MyPyramid was developed by the USDA as was the following "Dietary Guidelines for Americans." By following these guidelines, you can promote your health and reduce your risk for chronic diseases such as heart disease, certain cancers, diabetes, stroke, and osteoporosis. These diseases are leading causes of death and disability among Americans.

The "Dietary Guidelines for Americans" for your health and that of your family are:

Aim for fitness.

- Aim for a healthy weight.
- Be physically active each day.

Build a healthy base.

- Let the MyPyramid guide your food choices.
- Choose a variety of grains daily, especially whole grains.
- Choose a variety of fruits and vegetables daily.
- Keep food safe to eat.

Choose sensibly.

- Choose a diet that is low in saturated fat and cholesterol and moderate in total fat.

- Choose beverages and foods to moderate your intake of sugars.

- Choose and prepare foods with less salt.

- If you drink alcoholic beverages, do so in moderation.

Your Digestive System

Knowing what is in your food is only part of the story for understanding how nutrition relates to being healthy and fit. You also need to know how the nutrients in the food you eat get all around your body. You know that you can't just rub a piece of meat on your arm and build muscle tissue. Somehow the nutrients in that meat, or in any other food you eat, need to get inside your body in a useful form. This process is called **digestion**. Digestion is performed by your **digestive system** and has four major steps.

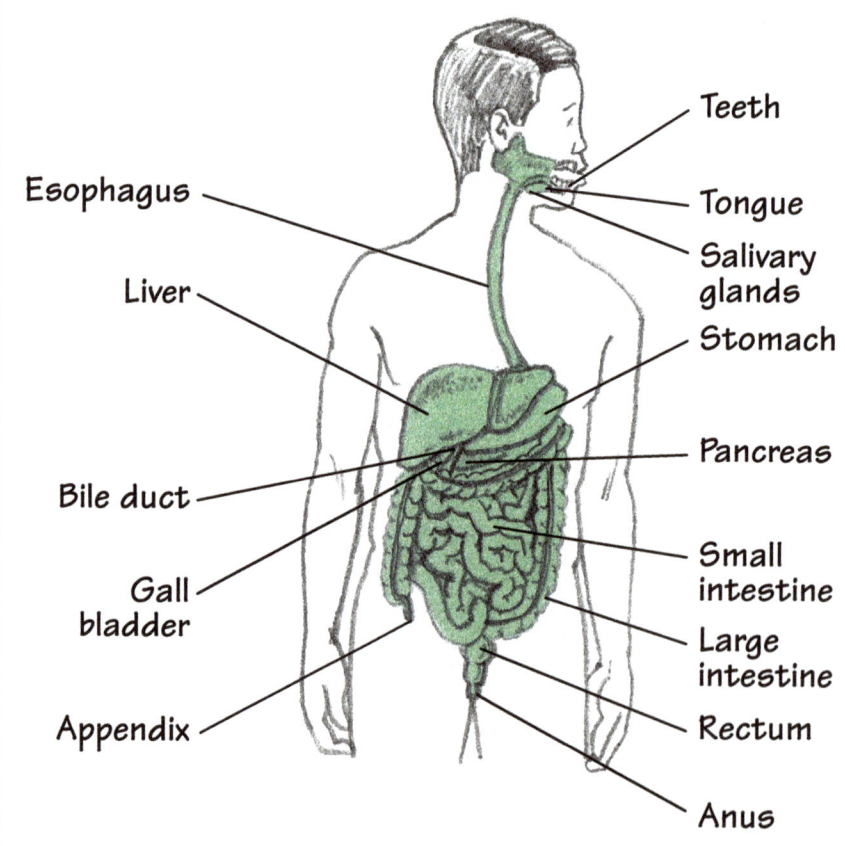

1. Getting food inside is to put it into your mouth. When food is in your mouth, you chew it and begin breaking it into smaller pieces. In addition to this mechanical breakdown by your teeth, your **saliva** (spit) also helps break down your food chemically. (Saliva comes from your **salivary glands**.)

2. Then you swallow the food you have chewed. The food goes down your **esophagus** into your **stomach**. In the stomach, a strong acid (a chemical) mixes with the food and breaks it down into a liquid mush.

3. This liquid mush then moves into the **small intestine**, where it mixes with more body chemicals. After this mixing, the nutrients in the food you ate are in a form that can help your body. The nutrients are absorbed from the small intestine into the bloodstream. Did you know that an adult's small intestine is almost 22 feet (7 meters) long?

4. Digestion occurs in the **large intestine**. The large intestine compacts the solids that are left after your bloodstream absorbs the nutrients. Then your body absorbs the water from these solids and eliminates the compacted solids as waste. Fiber in your food helps move this waste through your digestive system quickly and regularly.

The digestive system is a very important part of maintaining physical fitness. All the energy and nutrients needed by the body are processed by this system. Then the cardiovascular system acts like a highway system to transport the nutrients and energy wherever your body needs them. (The cardiovascular system is also called your **circulatory system** because it circulates the blood throughout your body.) The digestive system, in combination with the cardiovascular system, moves nutrients around your body to help your bones, skin, hair, and nails grow and your cells work the way they should.

✓ Checking Understanding

Part A: Talk about the following questions with your teammates. Then write your own response to each question in your notebook.

1. How would you plan healthy meals and snacks if you were in charge of planning the meals for your family? Plan the meals and snacks for your family for two days. Make sure that your decisions meet the guidelines set by the USDA (MyPyramid and "Dietary Guidelines for Americans").

2. How does the digestive system get nutrients from food into your body?

3. How do the digestive and cardiovascular systems work together?

4. At the beginning of the lesson, you talked about the statement, "You are what you eat." What does that statement mean to you now?

Part B: Review the "Doing Science" section on pages 1–9. Look at the graphic organizer on page 2. Talk about ways that you were doing science during this lesson. Then, on your own, describe ways in which you were doing science in your notebook.

Part C: Think about the activities that you did and the strategies that you used during this lesson. Talk about the following questions with your teammates. Then write your own response to each question in your notebook.

1. What did you learn during this lesson?

2. What activities or strategies helped you learn? How or why were they helpful?

3. Did working as a team help you learn? Why or why not?

4. What skills did your team do well? What skills does your team need to improve?

Lesson 7

My Plans for Fitness

Remember Muscle Powder from lesson 1? Now do you believe it would help someone become more fit? It takes much more than a magic powder to make you physically fit. Apply what you have learned to make a fitness plan. Remember the cardinal rule: fitness should be fun!

A Review of Overall Fitness

When you have **cardiovascular endurance**, you will not get out of breath as quickly as you would if you were not fit. Having a fit heart reduces a person's chances of having a heart attack or a stroke—two major killers of adults. Aerobic exercises, those that exercise the heart and lungs, also help control the amount of fat on a person's body. Aerobic exercises use a lot of energy.

Muscle strength is important to everyone. If your muscles are strong, you can lift and move things easily. Strong muscles can also protect a person from injury. You can strengthen your muscles only by using them! You can build strong muscles through all kinds of activities, including exercises like push-ups and sit-ups.

When you have **muscular endurance**, you can work and play for a long time before your muscles get tired. Boys and girls your age can increase their muscle endurance by repeating certain movements. To increase your muscle

endurance, you need to overload them slightly, just enough that they become tired but not injured. The best way to overload your muscles is to do a lot of repetitions using the same muscles, like riding your bicycle.

If you are **flexible**, you can move your muscles and joints freely. Flexibility also reduces injuries. Joint movement and stretching exercises improve flexibility and help relieve tension and stress.

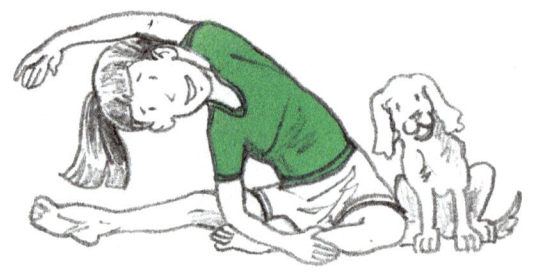

Remember MyPyramid? It showed that a healthy diet is mainly from the following three groups: the bread, cereal, rice, and pasta group (especially whole-grain foods); the vegetable group; and the fruit group. You also need foods from the milk, yogurt, and cheese group and the meat, poultry, fish, dry beans, eggs, and nut group, but not as many servings each day. Eating a balanced diet that is low in fats, sugar, and sodium is an important part of being fit.

Another important part of fitness is maintaining a **lean body**. A lean body is not necessarily a small, thin body. A lean body has enough fat for warmth, for protection of internal organs, and for padding, but does not have a lot of extra fat. Extra fat makes the body work harder. Moving the extra weight takes energy. Regular exercise builds muscles and uses energy and will help make your body lean and firm.

These are the parts of overall fitness. If you participate regularly in physical activities and eat a healthy diet, you will feel good, look good, and have the energy you need for fun and daily activities.

Body Composition

One way you can maintain a lean body is to burn as many calories as you take in. What is a **calorie**? Technically, a calorie is the amount of heat it takes to raise the temperature of 1 gram of water 1 degree Celsius. All you really need to know to maintain a calorie balance is that calories are measures of **energy** and that energy is stored in food.

You get the energy you need by eating and digesting food. All foods and drinks, except water, have calories. Some foods have a lot of calories; others have very few. Your body uses, or "burns," the calories you get from food during all your daily activities, including sleeping. Some activities, such as running, burn a lot of calories. Some activities, such as watching television, don't burn many at all. All the calories you take in are available for you as energy. If you don't use them, they are stored for later use. Unused calories are stored in your body as fat.

Here are some general tips about maintaining a lean body and keeping your body fat in check.

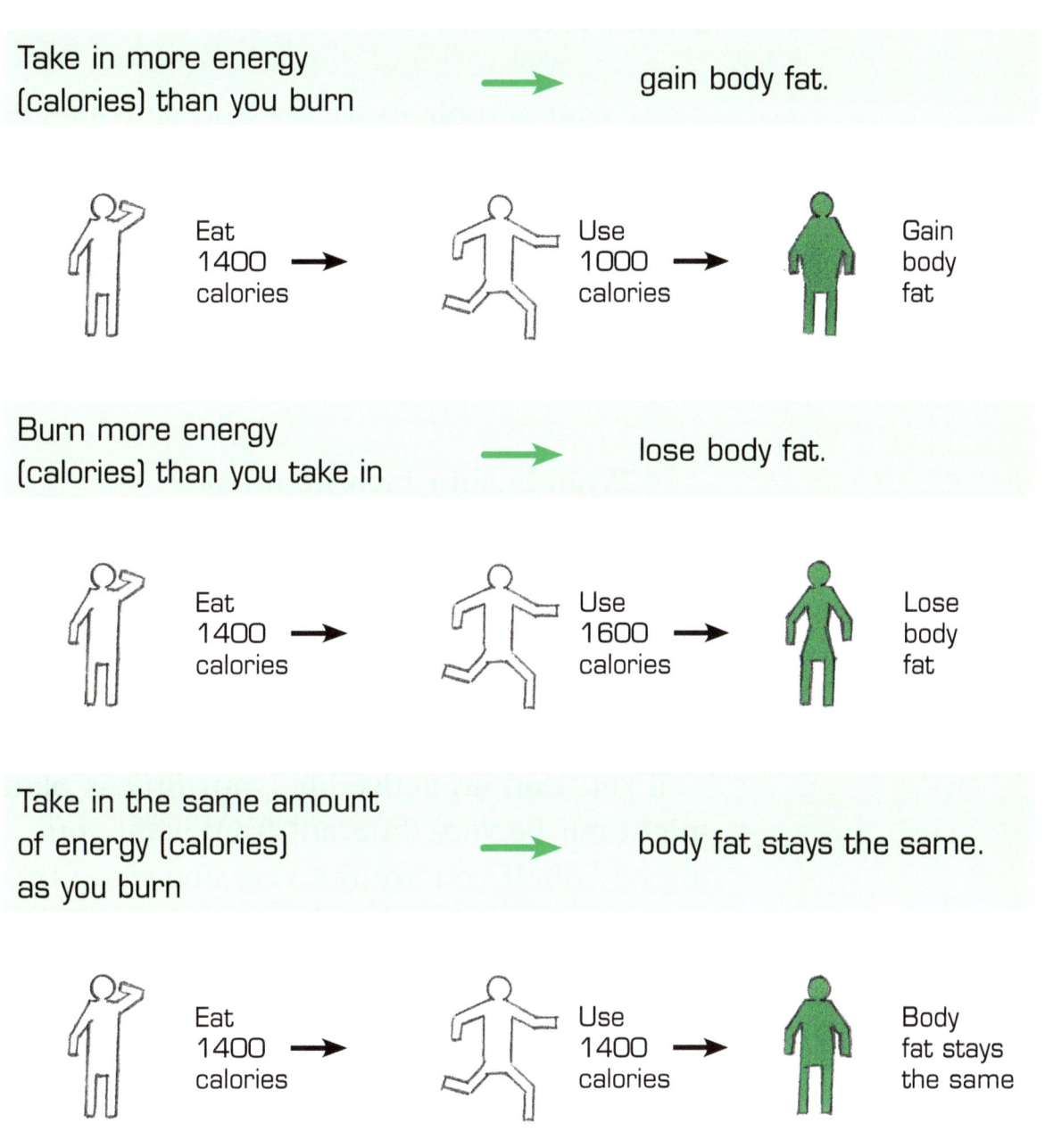

Evaluate

Making a Fitness Plan

If you want to become more fit, there are two things to do—get active and eat right! One way to help yourself get active is to make a fitness plan. Think about these questions to help you get started:

- What aerobic exercises and activities do you like to do?

- What stretching exercises do you like to do?

- Where do you like to exercise?

- What is your favorite music?

- Who is someone you would like to exercise with?

- How healthy are your eating habits?

If you lead an active life, your fitness plan might not be very different from what you already do. If you are not very active, a fitness plan could mean some changes in your lifestyle. If you aren't very active, remember to begin slowly and build up to fitness.

Team Task

Create a fitness plan that includes exercise and a healthy diet. Make sure it is a plan you can and will do!

Team Jobs

Tracker

Messenger

Skill Builder

Team Skills

Criticize ideas, not people

Team Supplies

- each teammate's notebook
- 3 wristbands
- 3 pencils

Directions

Note: Even though you are working in a team, you will develop your own fitness plan. Everyone might not want to do exactly the same activities or eat the same foods, but you can help one another develop your plans.

1. Make a "Fitness plan chart" in your notebook. You should make a plan for one week. It might look something like the following.

Day	Flexibility (warm-up)	Aerobic activities	Muscular strength and endurance	Flexibility (cool-down)	A healthy diet

If it is easier, you can make two charts—one for activities and one for a healthy diet.

2. Using the "Exercise Appendix" on pages 149–165, choose activities and exercises that you like to do. Write them in your "Fitness plan chart."

   - A warm-up exercise is one that warms up and gently stretches your muscles and joints. These exercises or activities start slowly and gradually increase in intensity to "warm up" your heart too and raise your heart rate a little.

   - The aerobic activities should be activities that you like to do that will keep your heart beating at a fast rate steadily for at least 20 minutes. Fast walking is one of the safest, easiest, and most effective aerobic exercises for people of all ages.

Make sure you choose activities and exercises for all the parts of fitness.

- When you choose exercises and activities for muscular strength and endurance, try to exercise all your major muscle groups sometime during the week. You need to do exercises or activities that strengthen your legs, your upper body and arms, your abdomen, and your back.

- Choose two or three cool-down exercises to complete your routine. These exercises should be a combination of slow aerobic exercise, such as slow walking, and gentle stretching. The slow aerobic exercise gradually brings your heart rate back down, and the stretching increases your muscle flexibility. The stretching prevents soreness and injuries. Hold each stretch for at least 15 seconds to stretch out your muscles completely. Remember not to bounce, but to stretch gently as far as you can without straining.

3. Now list foods that you would be willing to eat during the week that help you meet the guidelines for a healthy diet.

   a. Review MyPyramid on page 119 and the "Dietary Guidelines for Americans" on pages 121–123.

   b. Make sure to include foods you like to eat.

4. Review your fitness plan with your teacher.

5. Take your "Fitness plan chart" home and share it with your family members.

   a. Try to convince your family members to do the plan with you.

   b. Offer to help with the grocery shopping so you can stick with your plans for a healthy diet.

On Your Own

Carrying Out Your Fitness Plan

Part A: Thinking Ahead

Be sure to develop a plan that you can carry out. Sometimes you might have good intentions, but don't follow through. Think about these questions to help you carry out your fitness plan. Write answers in your notebook.

1. Who might exercise or be active with you? List at least two friends or family members whom you can call or invite to get active with you.

2. What might keep you from carrying out your plan? Your reasons could be things like these: "My parents won't let me ride my bike very far from home if I am alone. None of my friends like to ride bikes." Or "It costs money to go skating and I never have enough money." Or "Sometimes I want to jog around the track at school, but I am too embarrassed to do it by myself."

3. What might motivate you to carry out your plan? Your motivators could be things like: "If I did a few more chores around the house, then my parents might raise my allowance and I would have money to go skating." Or "If I called my friends ahead of time, one of them would ride bikes with me after school." Try to be realistic about what will help you carry out your plan.

Is your plan realistic?

Part B: Follow Through

Now carry out your fitness plan for one week. Get your family and friends to help you.

1. Pay attention to how your body feels.

   a. Is your heart beating faster during exercise?

   b. Is your breathing rate faster as you exercise?

   c. Are your muscles getting tired?

   d. Are you stretching gently and not straining your muscles?

   e. Are you having fun?

2. Record something in your notebook every day about how you feel after you exercise and eat a healthy diet.

   a. How long does it take before you feel a change?

   b. Pay attention to your heart rate, breathing rate, and muscles. How does your body change as you exercise?

✓ Checking Understanding

Throughout this module, you have been exploring systems of the body and how those systems can become more fit by exercising and eating right. By carrying out your fitness plan, you gained personal experience about what happens to your body during exercise and when you eat a healthy diet.

Part A: Talk about the following questions with your teammates. Then write your own response to each question in your notebook.

1. What is the difference between exercise and fitness? How does one help the other?

2. What will happen to your cardiovascular, respiratory, and musculoskeletal systems as you carry out your fitness plan? (Write about what the systems do as you exercise. You also can write about how the systems might change after you carry out your plan for one week.)

3. What did you learn about your body that you didn't know before? Write at least three things.

4. What questions about exercise, fitness, or your body systems would you like to answer now? Write at least two questions.

Part B: Review the "Doing Science" section on pages 1–9. Look at the graphic organizer on page 2. Talk about ways that you were doing science during this lesson. Then, on your own, describe ways in which you were doing science in your notebook.

Part C: Think about the activities that you did and the strategies that you used during this lesson. Talk about the following questions with your teammates. Then write your own response to each question in your notebook.

1. What did you learn during this lesson?

2. What activities or strategies helped you learn? How or why were they helpful?

3. Did working as a team help you learn? Why or why not?

4. What skills did your team do well? What skills does your team need to improve?

Exercise Appendix

The following pages contain descriptions of a variety of exercises or activities. The exercises or activities are divided into categories so that you can find exercises that help you develop flexibility, muscular strength and endurance, and cardiovascular endurance. Remember to start any workout with warm-up exercises and end with cool-down exercises. Be kind to your body and have fun becoming fit!

Warm-Up Exercises for Flexibility

Exercise 1: Who's There?

Slowly breathe in through your nose. Hold your breath for two to three seconds. Slowly blow out through your mouth. Repeat this breathing exercise 10 times.

Exercise 2: Wrist Circles

Hold your hands out to your sides with your elbows straight. Move both hands in circles. Do not move your arms. Make 10 forward circles. Make 10 backward circles.

Exercise 3: Windmills

Raise one arm straight up and leave your other arm straight down by your side. Move both arms around in circles as if you were a windmill. Make your arms go completely around 10 times. Reverse directions and make 10 more circles with your arms.

Exercise 4: Look Around

Look over your shoulder as far as you can to the right. Slowly move your head and look over your left shoulder. Look straight ahead. Repeat five times. Look straight ahead. Stop if you feel dizzy.

Exercise 5: Shoulder Talk

Turn to a partner. Raise one shoulder and begin the question, "How are you ...?" Lower that shoulder and raise the other shoulder. Complete the question, "... today? I ask." Lower that shoulder. Raise both shoulders in a shrug as if to say, "I don't know." Turn to another partner and repeat. Do this exercise five times. Variation: You could include the partner's name and say, "How are you, _____, today? I ask."

Exercise 6: The Bends

Put your hands over your head. Clasp your hands. Lean to the right. Feel your side stretch. Lean to the left. Feel your other side stretch. Repeat 10 times on each side.

Exercise 7: Stick 'Em Up

Bend your elbows so your hands rest on your shoulders. Raise both arms until they are straight up over your head. Stretch. Return your arms to your shoulders. Repeat 10 times.

Exercise 8: Do the Twist

Bend your elbows and put your hands in front of you. Twist your upper body to the right as far as you can comfortably go. As you twist, rotate on your toes and bend your knees slightly. Then twist to the left. Move slowly, but keep moving. Repeat 10 times.

Exercise 9: Crossed Knees

While standing, raise one knee up toward your chest. With your hands on the back of the thigh, pull your knee as close to you as you can. Hold it. Let go and lower your leg so your legs are crossed. Hold it. Bring the other knee to your chest. Repeat with each knee 10 times.

Exercise 10: Ankle Cross

Sit in a chair. Straighten one leg so your foot is off the floor. Make 10 circles to the right with that foot. Do not move your leg. Make 10 circles to the left with the same foot. Repeat with the other leg and foot. Variation: Spell your first name with your right foot, your last name with your left foot.

Exercise 11: Walk

Go to the gym or another large area you have chosen. Walk briskly.

Exercises for Muscular Strength

Arms and Upper Body

Exercise 12: Hand Squeezes

Hold your arms straight out to the side. Make a tight fist with both hands; hold five to 10 seconds; open your hands. Do this at least 10 times.

Exercise 13: Weight Lifter

Stand with your feet shoulder width apart and your back straight. Grasp a book in each hand. Place a book on each shoulder. Using only your arm muscles, lift the books straight over your head. (If you cannot do this comfortably, get lighter books.) Return the books to your shoulders. Repeat 10 times.

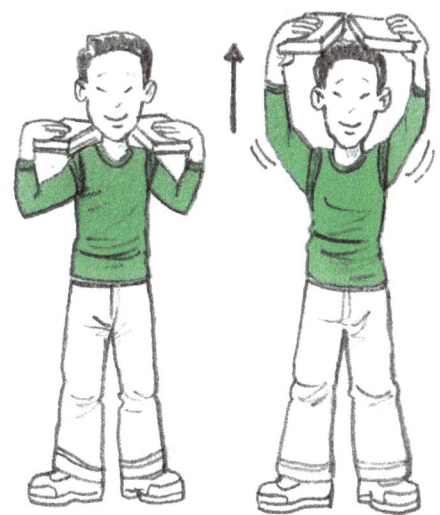

Exercise 14: Going Flying

Start with your hands at your sides. Keep your elbows straight and raise your arms out to your sides to shoulder height. Lower your arms. Flap your arms up and down 20 times.

Exercise 15: Coffee Grinder

Support your body on its side with one hand, one arm, and both feet. Walk your body in a circle using your supporting arm as a pivot. Change sides. Repeat the exercise five times on each side.

Exercise 16: Modified Push-Ups

Lie with your stomach on the ground. Put your hands, palms down, under your shoulders. Keep your knees on the ground and your back straight as you push up with your arms. Bend your arms and go back down, but do not touch the ground with your chest. Do as many push-ups as you can.

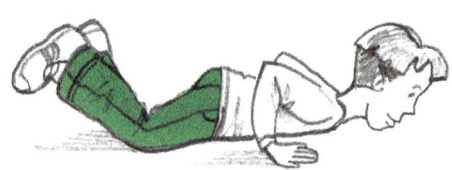

Exercise 17: Arm Circles

Hold your arms out at your sides. Keep your elbows straight. Move your arms from the shoulders to make forward circles. Repeat 10 times. Reverse and make backward circles. Repeat 10 times.

Abdomen

Exercise 18: Suck in That Gut

As you stand straight, pull your stomach in and try to touch your back with it. Hold it for a count of 10. Release and repeat at least five times.

Exercise 19: Tilt

Lie on your back with your knees bent and your feet flat on the floor. Press the lower part of your back to the floor and hold for five seconds. Relax. Repeat 10 times.

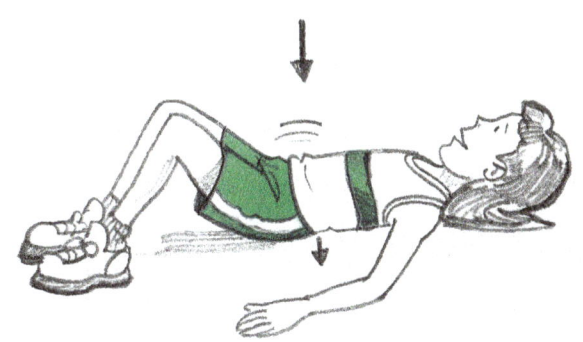

Exercise 20: Curl It Up

Lie on your back with your knees bent and feet flat on the floor. Cross your hands over your chest. Curl your upper body forward and up until your shoulders come up off the floor. Hold for five seconds. Return your shoulders to the floor. Repeat five times.

Exercise 21: Sideways Curls

Lie on your back with your knees bent and feet flat on the floor. Cross your left leg over your right knee. Place your hands behind your head so that your fingertips are just behind your ears. Twist your body forward and up so that your right shoulder faces your left knee. (Do not pull on your neck and head to lift yourself; use your stomach—abdominal—muscles.) Return to the floor. Repeat five times on each side.

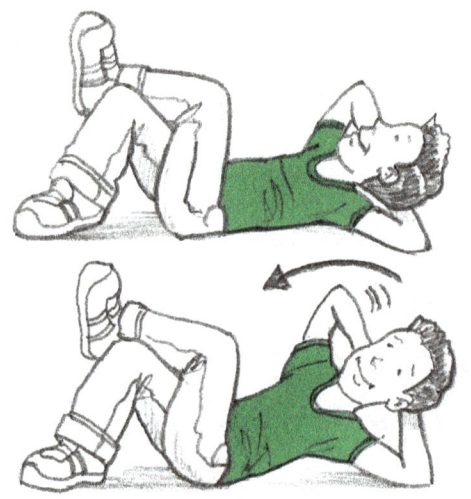

Legs

Exercise 22: Lunges

Take a long step forward with one leg and keep the other leg straight. Bend the knee of the front leg and lean forward so your weight is over that foot. Hold that position for three seconds. Straighten the front leg as you bring the rear leg forward. Repeat with the other leg in front. Do this 10 times.

Exercise 23: Side Leg Swings

Stand on your left leg. Swing your right leg to the right side until your right foot is at knee level. Bring your right foot back to the ground. Repeat 10 times. Stand on your right leg. Swing your left leg to the side. Do this 10 times. As an alternative exercise, lie on your side and swing your top leg up and out.

Exercise 24: Leg Lifts

Sit on a chair. Do not tilt back or rock it. Be sure you have room in front of you to stretch your legs out straight. Put your hands by your sides. Lift one leg. Keep your leg straight. Hold it and count to 10. Lower your leg. Raise your other leg and repeat. Do this leg-raising exercise five times.

Exercise 25: Stand Up, Sit Down

Sit on the edge of your chair. Put your hands slightly in front of you. Do not hold onto the chair. Stand up. Sit down. Repeat 10 times.

Exercise 26: Tiptoe Walk

Stand on tiptoe. Walk in place on your toes. Each time your left foot touches the floor, count. Take at least 10 steps. Then stand on your heels and lift your toes. Walk in place on your heels. Take at least 10 steps.

Exercise 27: Crab Walk

Sit on the floor. Put your hands and feet on the floor. Lift your rear and walk forward on your hands and feet five steps. Then walk backward five steps.

Exercise 28: Sitting on Air

Stand with your back against a wall and your heels 20 to 30 centimeters (8 to 12 inches) from the wall. Bend your knees and "sit." Hold that position for as long as you can. Try doing this exercise with a friend and chat while you are "sitting."

Aerobic Exercises for Cardiovascular Endurance

Exercise 29: March in Place

March in place, bringing your knees up high. Every time your left foot touches the floor, count. Take at least 60 steps. Add your own arm movements.

Exercise 30: Jog in Place

Jog in place. Each time your left foot touches the floor, count. Take at least 60 steps. Add your own arm movements.

Exercise 31: Imaginary Rope Skipping

Pretend to hold a jump rope in your hands. Turn your hands as if you were turning a rope, and jump when the rope would be by your feet. Try jumping with both feet, jumping with one foot and then the other, or taking double jumps. Jump at least 15 times.

Exercise 32: Side Step

Take one step to the right; then bring your left foot to your right foot. Take one step to the left and bring your right foot to your left. Repeat stepping to each side at least 30 times.

Exercise 33: Sit and Jog

Pick one person to be the leader. Sit in a chair. Move your legs and arms as if you were jogging. When the leader says something that applies to you, get up and jog around the room once. Return to your seat and keep jogging in place while you are sitting. The leader might say, "Everyone who owns a pet, move." "Everyone who has brown eyes, move." "Every girl, move." "Everyone who has a brother, move." "Everyone who ate candy or chips for lunch, move." "Everyone who flossed this morning, move."

Exercise 34: Rock-a-Bye

Put one foot in front of the other. Hop forward and backward from one foot to the other foot 10 times. Then put the first foot next to the other foot. Hop from side to side 10 times. Repeat the exercise, adding your own arm motions. Continue hopping for at least a minute.

Exercise 35: Tag

Choose one or more of these variations of tag.

- Shadow Tag. Everyone is "it" and tries to step on the shadows of others, while avoiding others stepping on his or her shadow.

- Elbow-Linked Tag. Everyone should link elbows with a partner except the two or three people who are "it." If "it" links elbows with someone, that person becomes "it." (Designate at least one girl and one boy as "it.")

- Aerobic Tag. Select one or more volunteers to be "it." To avoid being tagged, a person stoops as "it" gets close, but at the same time the person must name an aerobic activity. Failure to name an aerobic activity means the person may be tagged and then becomes "it."

- Triad Tag. (Divide the class into groups of four.) In each group, one person is "it," two people are protectors, and one person is the protected who can be tagged by the one who is "it." The protectors and the protected join hands to form a line. The protected is in the middle, and the protectors are at the ends. If "it" tags the protected, one of the protectors becomes "it," and the other becomes the protected. "It" and the protected become protectors.

Exercise 36: Snake's Tail

(Divide into two or three teams of six to 10 students per team.) Each group lines up. Each teammate holds on to the waist of the person in front of him or her. The snake's head tries to catch the snake's tail. The tail tries to avoid being caught. If the head grabs the tail's waist, the head becomes the new tail and the second in line becomes the new head. Variation: One team's snake's head can try to catch another team's snake's tail.

Cool-Down Exercises for Flexibility

Exercise 37: The Cat

Sit on a chair. Put your chin on your chest, round your back, and reach down and hold your ankles. Hold for a count of 10. Sit up by straightening your back, then your shoulders, and finally your head. Repeat 10 times.

Exercise 38: Chair Lift

Sit on a chair and hold the seat with both hands. Try to lift the chair while you are sitting on it. Then try to lift yourself off the chair's seat while pushing down on the chair. Repeat five times.

Exercise 39: Knee Lift

Sit on a chair and place your hands on the back of the thigh of one leg. Lift that leg to your chest so that your knee is near your chest. Hold for a count of 10. Put your leg down and repeat with the other leg. Do this exercise five times.

Exercise 40: Elbow to Knee

Put your hands behind your head and clasp them. Lift one knee. Touch your knee with your elbow of the opposite side. Lower your knee. Repeat with the other knee and elbow. Do this 10 times.

Exercise 41: Butterflies

Sit on the floor and put the soles of your feet together. With your hands, press your knees down until you feel a stretch in your legs. Hold this position for 10 seconds. Repeat five times.

Exercise 42: Side Stretch

Raise your left arm over your head. Lean to the right, but do not lean forward or backward. Hold this position for a count of five. Stand up straight. Repeat five times. Do the same exercise leaning to the left. Variation: Hold a book in the hand that is raised.

Exercise 43: Knee-High Stretch

Stand on one foot. The leg you are standing on should be bent slightly. Lift the knee of the other leg. Use the hand of the same side as the knee to pull the knee higher. Pull until you feel tightness in your leg. You may use your other hand for balance, if needed. Hold for five seconds. Repeat with the other leg. Repeat this exercise with each leg at least five times.

Exercise 44: Wall Push-Ups

Facing a wall, stand with your feet together about half a meter from the wall. Place both hands on the wall. Bend your elbows as you keep your body straight and your heels on the floor. Stop bending your arms when you feel tightness in your legs. Hold for a count of 10. Straighten your arms. If you were unable to feel tightness before your face touched the walls, step a little farther from the wall. If your face did not reach the wall before you felt tightness, step closer to the wall. Repeat the push-ups five times.

Exercise 45: Pretzel Split

Sit on the floor. Put one leg straight in front of you. Put the heel of the other foot by your hip. Use both hands and reach for the toes on your straight leg. Hold for 10 seconds. Repeat five times. Put your legs in the opposite positions and repeat.

Glossary

aerobic exercise: An activity that requires the body to use oxygen for an extended period of time, usually 15 to 20 minutes.

air sac: One of the thin-walled microscopic pouches in which gases are exchanged in the lungs.

alveoli: Air sacs.

anaerobic: Without oxygen.

artery: A blood vessel that carries blood away from the heart.

atrium: One of the upper compartments of the heart.

brainstorm: A skill that teams use to think of a list of ideas before beginning an investigation or solving a problem.

bronchial tube: Tubes that branch off on the trachea.

bronchiole: A tiny thin-walled branch of a bronchial tube.

calorie: A measure of the energy value of foods, defined as the energy required to raise the temperature of 1 gram of water by 1 degree Celsius.

capillary: A tiny blood vessel.

cardiac: Something related to the heart.

cardiac muscle: The muscle that makes up your heart.

cardiovascular endurance: Being able to run and play without getting tired and out of breath.

cardiovascular system: Your heart, arteries, veins, capillaries, and blood.

circulatory system: Your heart, arteries, veins, capillaries, and blood.

claim: A statement that someone wants you to think is true.

contract: Muscles become shorter and fatter in order to pull bone.

data: Information collected in a scientific investigation.

diaphragm: The muscle beneath your lungs.

digestion: The process of changing food that has been eaten into a form that can be used in the body.

digestive system: The parts of your body that function together to digest food.

direct evidence: Evidence you collect yourself.

endurance: The ability to do something for a long time.

energy: The power or capacity to be active.

esophagus: The tube that leads from your throat to your stomach.

exercise: To move or put into action.

exhale: To breathe out.

fitness: In good health.

flexible: Being able to move your muscles and joints freely.

healthy diet: Food that is good for your body.

heart rate: How fast your heat beats in one minute.

indirect evidence: Evidence that you do not collect yourself, but rely on evidence collected by others.

inhale: To breathe in.

joint: A place where bones are joined.

large intestine: The place where solid wastes are compacted after nutrients have been absorbed by your body.

lean body: Having enough, but not extra, fat.

lung: One of two baglike organs that allow you to breathe.

materials manager: Has the team job of getting the supplies that are listed in the "Team Supplies" section for each lesson; when the team task is completed, the materials manager returns the supplies to the supply table.

messenger: Has the team job to ask another team's messenger or your teacher for help if the team gets stuck.

model: A copy or representation of something.

muscle endurance: Being able to use your muscles for long periods of time without them becoming tired.

muscle strength: Makes work and play easier.

musculoskeletal system: Your muscles and bones working together.

nasal passages: A chamber that lies between the floor of the skull and the roof of the mouth.

nutrient: The component of food that provides nourishment to the body.

prediction: A scientist's way of describing what he or she thinks will happen in an investigation based on what he or she already knows.

pulse: The "push" of blood against the walls of your arteries.

record: A writing, drawing, chart, or graph.

resistance exercise: Exercise that involves working your muscles against free weights or your body's own weight (for example, walking, running, and push-ups).

respiratory system: The organs that work as a system to allow someone to breathe.

saliva: The watery fluid that forms in your mouth; spit.

salivary glands: The organs that produce saliva.

skeletal muscle: The muscle that is connected to bones. It allows you to move and be active.

skeleton: Your body framework.

skepticism: Not believing everything that you read or hear, but questioning it.

skill builder: Has the job of encouraging teammates to practice the team skills.

small intestine: The place where nutrients are absorbed into your bloodstream.

smooth muscle: The muscle found in organs of the body such as the stomach, the lungs, and the kidneys.

steroid: A muscle drug.

stomach: The pouch where food goes after it leaves the esophagus; while in the stomach, strong acids mix with food to break it down into a liquid mush.

tracker: Has the team job of keeping track of what the team is doing and makes sure the team does every step and follows the directions in order.

trachea: The main part of the system of tubes by which air passes to and from the lungs – known also as windpipe.

vein: A blood vessel that carries blood to the heart.

ventricle: One of the two lower compartments of the heart.

Acknowledgments

Photo credits:

Carlye Calvin: p. 39 (top left); p. 39 (top right); p. 39 (bottom left); p. 39 (bottom right); p. 62

Comstock: p. 3 (left); p. 8 (right); p. 101

Corbis: p. 8 (left)

Eyewire: p. 3 (right)

Life Art: p. 77 (lower right)

iStockphoto: p. 9 (right); p. 77 (left)

PhotoDisc: p. 4 (left); p. 5 (right); p. 7 (right); p. 9 (left); p. 131

Shutterstock: p. 1; p. 6 (left); p. 6 (right)

Special thanks to the administration, teachers, students, and parents of Vineland Elementary, Pueblo, Colorado, for allowing us to photograph students "doing science": p. 18

Text Credits

"The Respiratory System" on pp. 92-97. Special permission granted by *Current Health* Magazine, published by Field Publications. Copyright © 1990 by Field Publications. *Current Health* is a federally registered trademark of Field Publications.

"Steroids: Muscle Madness" on pages 48-49: "Ask Mr. Muscles" © 1998 by Consumers Union of U.S., Inc., Yonkers, NY 10703-1057, a nonprofit organization. Reprinted with permission from the February/March 1988 issue of *Zillions* (formerly Penny Power) for educational purposes only. No commercial use or photocopying permitted. To subscribe, call 1-800-234-2078.

Cover Credits:

© 2006 JupiterImages Corporation: back cover Literacy Collage (Reading and Writing)

Digital Vision: back cover Literacy Collage (Listening); front cover image

Image 100: back cover Literacy Collage (Speaking)

www.ingramcontent.com/pod-product-compliance
Ingram Content Group UK Ltd.
Pitfield, Milton Keynes, MK11 3LW, UK
UKHW051700240426
12048UKWH00046B/707